THE INVITATION

OF

Motherhood

Uncovering the Spiritual
Lessons of Parenting

Deborah McNamara

1st Edition

PERFORMANCE
INTEGRAL

Performance Integral Edition
Copyright © 2018

Published by Performance Integral, Boulder, Colorado.
www.PerformanceIntegral.com

FIRST EDITION

*Printed responsibly with the following sustainability
certifications:*
  Sustainable Forest Initiative® SFI®
  Endorsement of Forest Certification™ PEFC™
  Forest Stewardship Council® FSC®

2 4 6 8 10 9 7 5 3 1

Cover Art Design
by
A n u r u p   G h o s h

Editor-In-Chief ◆ Robin Quinn

LIBRARY OF CONGRESS CATALOGING-IN-PUBLICATION DATA

McNamara, Deborah C.   1976 -
  The Invitation of Motherhood, Uncovering The Spiritual Lessons
of Parenting / Deborah McNamara

ISBN-10: 0-9887689-4-1
ISBN-13: 978-0-9887689-4-9

  (Softcover)

  1. Parenting. 2. Spirituality. 3. Women's Interest. 4. Narrative
  Non-Fiction 5. Self-Help.

Library of Congress Control Number: 2018939286

For Rowan, Braeden and Kienan,
who have taught me so much.

And for mothers everywhere, acknowledging that the path to becoming a mother is varied and wide. Whether you are a birth mother, a mother through adoption, an egg-donor mother, a foster mother, or a woman without her own children still 'mothering' in other ways, this book is dedicated to you and to all the unseen gestures you undertake day in and day out that serve this world. Thank you.

"The One who we adore as the Mother is the divine conscious force that dominates all existence, one and yet so many-sided that to follow her movement is impossible even for the quickest mind...Universal, she creates all beings and contains and enters, supports and conducts a million processes and forces.

If you desire transformation put yourself in the hands of the Mother without resistance and let her do unhindered her work within you. Three things you must have: consciousness, plasticity, and unreserved surrender. Follow your soul and not your mind: your soul that answers to truth."

~ Sri Aurobindo, *The Mother*

Contents

Part IV. Working with Difficult Emotions

Part V. Love Is a Practice

Part VI. Taking Pause: Making Time to Live into the Good Stuff

Foreword

by

Miriam Mason Martineau

The book you hold in your hands is a remarkable account of one woman's journey into and through motherhood. Part memoir, part teachings, reflective invitations, poetry, and prayer, this book is of earth and of spirit. It embraces both the diapers and the stars. Both the excruciating and the exhilarating. The deeply personal and the vastly universal. The mundane, the practical, the mystical and the extraordinary. Space is made for all of it.

I am delighted to welcome you to an exploration and conversation that often takes place only in the most private recesses of a mother's heart, mind and body. In a deeply honest collection of reflections on motherhood, Deborah McNamara offers insight and inspiration by sharing her questions, her struggles, as well as her discoveries and answers. She pays such close attention to her interior experience, that we are gifted with a rare glimpse into the inner workings, the challenges and opportunities mothers face, wrestle with and are awed by. In addition, we receive the added benefit of her experiences as they come to us sifted and sorted through her fine intelligence and generous heart.

While this book follows one mother's journey— Deborah McNamara's—her story goes far beyond her own experience. What she describes is indeed her unique, deeply personal account, but she speaks of an offering, of an opportunity and potential that is presented to each and every mother. It is the possibility of being transformed, changed for the better, through the daily (and nightly!) act of mothering.

In my experience, the most profound and lasting kind of transformation usually happens in relationship. This is where the rubber hits the road. It is not on the meditation cushion, or in a cave, chapel or temple. It is in the messy wildness of relational life. Relationship is where we are ultimately tested, where we find out if our transformation and growth actually stick. Add the particular dynamic of the parent-child and you have a unique constellation: an unequal one. You are the one asked to surrender, not your child. You are asked to carve yourself out, to make space, to pay more attention to another than to yourself. It can sound crazy as an ask, and yet, it holds in it a secret to true transformation: to be pushed beyond your normal comfort zones, to pour yourself out for an other, to be in service to the well-being of someone utterly dependent on you, and ultimately, to make love bigger than anything and anyone that crosses your path, particularly your child.

Yes, raising a child is an act of service beyond yourself. It is an act that leads you well outside your familiar territory, into the uncertain, into ongoing change. How wonderful to have someone like Deborah share the gems she has both been graced with as well as worked hard to discover. Her insights are not glib or quickly found. You reap here the wisdom that Deborah has tested, tried and challenged on the soils of ongoing exhaustion, never-ending piles of laundry, frequent squabbles and messes amongst siblings, as well as the ground of the greatest love and joy possible: the love for a child, for life unfolding before her very eyes.

This book will help you find balance amidst the ever-shifting sands of parenthood. As you follow her curiosity and courage, you will discover:

Practical ways onward and forward—how mothers can cope with new stressors; how to work with difficult moments that arise with your child(ren); how to respond with love and compassion when stretched beyond your perceived limits; how to stay focused on connection during and after the stormy times of upheaval and conflict.

Spiritual lessons embedded in the motherhood journey. You will read about how motherhood changes you and offers opportunity for personal and spiritual growth. You will also discover how spiritual insight can be incredibly practical, for example, in the realm of discipline, whereby children are encouraged to be loved and become Love: to be accommodated and learn to adapt to the needs of others.

Deborah McNamara's book will also offer you a welcoming sense of kinship—you are not alone. As someone who has been researching, practicing and teaching *Parenting as a Spiritual Practice* for over 20 years, I am thankful for this beautifully written and moving example of just that, in action. Deborah is engaging her parenting as a viable, relevant and highly effective spiritual practice, and she invites you to join her. She encourages you, gently, to become the most wonderful you possible. To loosen the ties to your separate self over and over again, by being nudged, and yes, sometimes forced to just: let go. To let your attachment to sleep go. To let your attachment to your former body shape or former professional self or independence or identity or former "fill-in-the-blank" go. To let go of your conditioned reactions that stubbornly want to lead the show - those knee-jerk outbursts and disgruntlements that you have made your own for so long that they actually feel like you. But don't worry - this is not a book about self-negating. It is not about letting go of sleep (!) or an invigorating career or a healthy self-image. Just the *attachment* to such. This is not a tale of a woman who has discarded her needs. On the contrary, Deborah McNamara digs deeper to discover what her truest needs are, and those she tends, she nurtures and waters like a plant emerging in the springtime. She shows you how her true Self has been there all along, how your true You is there all along too, and ready to be uncovered more fully in the crucible that is mothering. This is a journey for all of us to take. It is a human journey, the journey of becoming the fullest expression of our Self. And it is one that can be done effectively in and through the act of parenting.

"The antidote to exhaustion is not necessarily rest. The antidote to exhaustion is wholeheartedness."

~ Brother David Steindl-Rast

The invitation of motherhood Deborah speaks of is not the kind of mother-love that forgets the mother, but the kind that includes your mother-self in the bigger picture. You are transformed, not forgotten. You are changed from the inside out and from the outside in, and the change is toward a truer, fuller version of yourself. You are honed and evolved. Through parenting with awareness and compassion, your edges, your diamond-in-the-rough-self becomes more polished.

Mothering is one of the most important tasks on this planet. And parenting with the kind of presence and courage, and yes, also imperfection that Deborah suggests will change the future, child by child. It will enable children to grow up knowing how to regulate their emotions (rather than denying, repressing or over-indulging in them). It will help them know what it is to be loved and in their ways and in their time, to be loving. It will enable them to know in their bones that connection is stronger than conflict, and repair is always possible.

Enjoy this book! Dive in and let it change you. May it inspire you, offering you new breath and encouragement. May it support you in your own hearth and home, in your own journey through mothering, parenting, and relating.

~ Miriam Mason Martineau
Parenting Educator & Coach,
Mother, Counselor, Writer

Spring 2018
British Columbia, Canada

www.miriammartineau.com
www.integralparenting.com

Introduction

"The moment a child is born, the mother is also born. She never existed before. The woman existed, but the mother, never. A mother is something absolutely new."

~ Bhagwan Shree Rajneesh,
Indian Spiritual Teacher

Journeying into motherhood is not only marked by the birth of our children. It is also marked by our own birth into a new way of being. After my first son was born I felt my part in a long line of women bringing new life into this world. Being pregnant and giving birth led me to a massive opening of the body and the sense that this moment was one of the most profound given to our species: 280 days of gestation, the continued cycle of life, the evolution and propagation of humanity landing in our arms, a gift so precious we often call it a miracle.

Yet accompanying the quiet moments of awe was the dismay at how hard it felt. I had never been taken on such a ride of emotions and challenges. Why was it that everything I had read about becoming a mother was around preparing for birth and then how to parent (in practical terms) afterwards? I had read up on breastfeeding and the importance of choosing non-toxic crib mattresses. I had researched cloth diapers and read all the reviews of the compostable ones. I had read a book on the benefits of attachment parenting. I had perused at least 50 birth stories. After my first son's birth I looked for the fellow mothers writing about the deep inner processes at work during the transition into motherhood. I had a harder time than expected finding the words of wisdom that I so desperately needed.

Why wasn't there a 'motherhood' section at the bookstore? Why did it seem all the books fell into the categories of 'parenting advice' or 'how to?' Where were the writings on the vast spiritual lessons embedded in the motherhood journey? Where were the reflections on the ways in which our children call us to grow and transform? I wanted to know I wasn't alone. I wanted raw and unfiltered accounts of the difficult spaces we can enter into when pushed to our limits. How do other mothers cope with being up six times a night? How do mothers deal with difficult emotions while parenting? How do mothers deal with the loss of autonomy, the changes in body and moods, and the seemingly ceaseless demands for time and attention? And, perhaps most importantly, what were the lessons mothers were learning? How did motherhood spark growth and transformation?

While every year during a lifetime brings its changes, the year when one becomes a first-time mother is perhaps one of the most radical. Birth ushers in a space for profound transformation, coupled with physical discomfort, bliss and an often deep sense of fatigue—even if softened by the bond of parenthood. Immediately I was called to lose sleep, let go of many previous needs, and hand over my presence and attention to another being. Here was my first invitation to grow and change. During those early weeks and months, I was taken to unknown depths within myself. I met new limitations and greeted unexpected baggage from my past. I often felt I was in a hot crucible of transformation—where my child was the ever-present barometer of change.

The Invitation of Motherhood: A Spiritual Journey?

Luckily, a few books were there to offer perspective and insight into my new mother status. There was Karen Maezen Miller's *Momma Zen* and Andrea Buchanan's *Mother Shock*. There was *Literary Mama: Reading for the Maternally Inclined.* Yet, as the *Literary Mama* editors Andrea Buchanan and Amy Hudock suggest, most women's stories of personal growth after motherhood tend to remain untold. I wanted writing by mothers that captured the complexity and deeper inner processes at work. And I wanted to delve into how motherhood changes us and offers up opportunities for personal and spiritual growth.

I began to reflect on how motherhood was inviting me to become a better person. I also began to notice that the daily responsibilities and challenges of motherhood could be inviting me on the spiritual journey of a lifetime. I wanted to figure out how to bring mindfulness to each seemingly mundane moment of changing diapers, cleaning up messes, or mitigating ceaseless toddler and sibling conflicts. So I committed myself to be open to the lessons of mothering. I began paying close attention to my experience and made myself available to the insights that wanted to shine through.

I noticed that there were lessons to be learned and invitations to grow at every turn. There was the invitation to love unreservedly, even when tired.

There was the invitation to practice unwavering attention, even when scattered in a million directions. There was the invitation to let go of attachments to body and ego, and to embrace radical change wholeheartedly. In addition, there was the invitation to embrace humility in the face of those inevitable moments of challenge and testing. If I heeded these invitations, perhaps I could merge my deepest intentions in order to manifest the sanest, most grounded expression of what it means to be human.

So What Is This Book?

An early reader of this book asked me, "So what is this book? I can't tell if it is philosophy, spirituality, memoir or advice." The answer is that it is a bit of all of these things. In the following reflections, I share the honesty of my challenges, and the ways in which I have chosen to respond. I share the often poignant ways that my children, and the process of mothering them, have taught me some of the greatest lessons of life: how to love more deeply, how to be more present, and how to find compassion in the rough spaces. I share a rare glimpse into the inner processes at work while parenting, aiming to distill my experiences into tangible lessons learned. Throughout, my intention is to shed light on the opportunities for growth that I have experienced, while also giving voice to the often unspoken realms of exhaustion and difficulty that many of us mothers find ourselves in from time to time.

The Invitation of Motherhood was written in pieces during the early years of parenting my three young boys. Each section of the book speaks to a different aspect of my motherhood journey. In the following pages, I speak to the massive changes that were at play during my pregnancies and births, and the new "normal" that I encountered when tending hearth with my little ones in tow. I share the ways in which I coped when I was facing exhaustion, and how I made a commitment to practice love even when I was being stretched beyond what felt possible.

I have not shied away from delving into the difficult emotions that motherhood can evoke. It is true that "the moment a child is born, the mother is also born." Perhaps one of the most important invitations of motherhood has been to welcome the complexity of the experience. There is transition. There is infinite change. There is a new experience of love like no other. There is joy coupled with challenge. There are growing pains with a backdrop of bliss. Whatever your experience, I hope the reflections on these pages support your own motherhood journey and remind you of the infinite invitations beckoning in all moments.

PART I

Pregnancy, Birth & the Spaces In-Between

"In giving birth to our babies, we may find that we give birth to new possibilities within ourselves."

~ Myla and Jon Kabat-Zinn

Everyday Blessings: The Inner Work of Mindful Parenting

Each woman's journey to motherhood is marked by a significant transition. The word "threshold" comes to mind. It comes from an Old English word pointing to the practice of threshing (separating grain from a plant) outside the entrance to one's home. This was the space where women would gather and work, "threshing" just outside the doorway. Over time, that place before entry became known as a threshold - now connoting the space between one thing or place and another.

For many of us, when we cross the threshold into becoming a mother, the way in which we experience ourselves shifts. Our bodies change. Often, attachments or preferences for how we physically look and feel are revealed. For me, discomfort reigned - even amidst the joyful anticipation of welcoming a new life.

I became pregnant and gave birth three times. Each time I was offered up different insights to consider. There was the gift of waiting, even when I was anxious or impatient. There was the invitation to shed my skin - over and over again, even when I was fiercely resistant to change. Each birth humbled me to my own limitations, while also showing me my deepest strengths. And after I was silent and resting in bed with a newborn in my arms, I could reflect on my place in time—catching my breath in the midst of what is too often a busy sea of responsibility.

Each pregnancy and birth was like walking in and out of a labyrinth. I was embarking on an entirely new path. Each curve along the way afforded fresh insights. In Part I, I invite you to join me - perhaps anticipating (or remembering) your own unique journey to motherhood.

Shedding Our Skins, Even When Attached

Attach: from Old French, meaning "to attach, fix, stake up, support"; related to the Frankish word "stakon": a post or stake, and the Germanic word "stake": to fasten, affix or connect.

Pregnancy brought with it a series of confrontations with my attachments. It seemed no coincidence that the word "attachment" is related to a stake. Attachments are fierce. We stake our claims and hold to them. It also seemed no coincidence that attachments are historically related to property and the law. This is serious territory. Our attachments can be as strong as stakes in the ground, holding up a seemingly firm foundation. We can rest with the illusion that our attachments support us. We can be affixed to them.

Pregnancy had revealed my fierce attachment to my body as it was before I'd become a mother. I remember the moments in front of the mirror as I witnessed my body changing. As much as I wanted to embrace that my pregnant body was beautiful, that was hard. Each time I was weighed at a prenatal appointment, I cringed. How could this be? My firstborn was only five and a half pounds at birth, but after 41 weeks of gestation I'd gained fifty!

I was 32 years old and while elated, I was also mortified. The pounds were packing on just by looking at food. Fifty pounds and nine months later, I was feeling like a tub. I knew change was part of this process, but *50 pounds* of change? How could I even wrestle myself out of bed in the mornings? I lugged my new self around and tried with all my might to "trust the process," hard as that was. To boot, I was nauseous and tired. I had always been a sound sleeper but now I was up at 3am eating Spanish goat cheese (one of my recurring cravings). I kept telling myself to surrender, to "let go" (and all of the other simple wisdom clichés that emerged during pregnancy), but I was like a wheel stuck in mud. I wanted to go back to what was. I did *not* want to shed my skin and start anew.

I confessed to myself: I was attached to my non-pregnant (and pre-pregnant) state. I had been a figure skater and cross-country runner in my youth, and had always enjoyed movement. My 20s had been full of high altitude hikes in Oregon and Colorado. At age 25, I had found the practice of Hatha yoga and in recent years it had become a cornerstone in my life. I went on to become a yoga teacher and had been teaching for five years before my first son was born. While I understood that the deeper practice of yoga transcended how I moved on a mat, it still bothered me that my range of motion was limited as the pounds packed on. And, in spite of practicing an orientation of acceptance, I was still flummoxed by my rapidly expanding bodily form.

The experience of pregnancy was inviting me to face a lifetime's worth of bodily change condensed into 40 weeks: a wake-up call to how life and time work on us. It was a practice of transformation. Just like a snake shedding its skin—or a caterpillar becoming a butterfly in one of the most miraculous moments of metamorphosis—I was invited over and over again to open myself to the blessings of change.

We Are Fluid, Not Fixed

So there I was: pregnant and holding on to my attachments to what my body used to be as if holding on for dear life. I kept trying to remind myself that our bodies aren't fixed entities. Our identities aren't married to the outward shape of bodily form. Women especially are shapeshifters. Our bodies are vessels, conduits. We are fluid, not 'fixed.' Life is ultimately rooted in constant change, and pregnancy was turning out to be a crash course in the inevitability of transformation. It was also serving as a sound reminder of the ultimate inevitability of aging. And yet my attachment tendency kept trying to pull me to the illusion that who I really am is something apart from this presently nauseous, huge version of myself.

But why? Why was it so hard to identify with this glorious present moment of a huge baby belly? No matter how amazing I felt the process of pregnancy to be, I couldn't seem to break free from the trap of clinging to the notion that my identity was somehow static. I wanted to identify more with who I was "pre-pregnancy" or "post-pregnancy." I was resisting the changing body inherent in growing a baby. I disliked the heart burn, the steady weight gain, the pressure on bladder and stomach. I was clinging to what I was and what I hoped to return to as a norm after baby was born, even though I knew it wasn't a necessarily helpful aspiration.

There I was, teetering between my attachments and the invitation to embrace change and transcend my preferences. Pregnancy was showing me the lapses of where I wasn't comfortable in my own, changing skin. It was showing me where I falsely rested my identity. Vanity was revealed, and then obliterated.

A First Great Lesson of Motherhood

This was one of the first great lessons, and invitations, of motherhood. It began as a grim acceptance of the truth of impermanence - and the recognition that there is no "fixed" version of myself to orient around. The only constant is change. We are fluid, changing entities, interrelated, worked on, moved by life. There is nothing to return to and nowhere to go. There is nothing static. No stake to hold on to. No foundation to attach to. Pregnancy is a crash course in these insights at a fast forward pace. It is life's simultaneous decomposition accompanied by creativity and newness: A mother's bodily expansion and loosening coupled with a baby's slow growth into new expression of life. There is no return to anything but to the present moment of reality where each millisecond is a different expression of self and truth and body. *If we can relax attachments to who we think we are outside of the ever-shifting present moment, we can tap into the fluid expression of spontaneous awareness that has no limitations.*

Shedding the proverbial skin can be difficult. Fifty pounds of change can be difficult. The key for me was to not hold on too tightly to what has been, and to trust that I was leaving behind something equally lovely as the beauty and mystery of what was to come. This is the true realm of freedom, served up to us lucky mothers on a platter of 75 grams of protein a day.

The Invitation

Consider your own attachments.

How can you let go of what has been in order to be open to the blessings of change?

If letting go is difficult, practice gratitude for at least one thing that is new and different now.

No matter where you are in your motherhood journey, practice being comfortable in your own, changing skin.

The Gift of Waiting & the Spaces In-Between

"It was the tiniest thing I ever decided to put my whole life into."

~ Terri Guillemets, Author and Poet

It was July 12th, 2009 and I'd just given birth to my first son, Rowan. It was the full swing of summer - with sunflowers in full bloom and grasshoppers buzzing in the foothills behind my home. Rowan had been born at home at 5:26 am just as the sun was rising. The day was already hot and the midwives had been putting ice on my legs to cool me down after the long night of labor.

As I was holding my son and reflecting on his birth, my midwife said to me, "Don't you think ushering new life is going to bring you to your knees? It brings me to my knees every time." We'd been talking about my struggle to push Rowan into the world, and how the pain literally had brought me to my knees. At 1:26 am, I'd been fully dilated and ready to push. Little did I know at that moment that it would take a full four hours of pushing before he would be born.

Those brutal hours from 1:26 am to 5:26 am were unlike any other in my life. I was in what felt like a timeless portal, where I was afforded an unmistakable glimpse into the vast mystery of life. Those hours of pushing took me to places where I felt utterly out of control. Those hours of pushing were vexing yet awe-inspiring, bringing me to my knees in a gesture of humility so all-consuming it took my breath away again and again. There was no way out but in. No turning away or back. The threshold of birth had to be crossed.

The Spaces In-Between

Each of my three pregnancies and births served as a unique threshold in my life. The word liminal came to mind each time: *a transitional or initial stage of a process, occupying a position at, or on both sides of, a boundary or threshold.* Pregnancy seemed a perfect time to settle into the mystery of liminality. I choose intentionally to hang in the spaces in-between. It was like swinging freely in the balance of the inner and outer, the inside world and outside, much like the womb contrasted by the vast space of everything else. It felt like walking the thin lines between darkness and light, mystery and the known, fullness and release, contraction and expansion.

Before the word "pregnant" meant "with child," it actually meant "full of meaning." I often found myself reflecting on this, trying to remember the gifts embedded in liminal spaces, and the gift of resting in a period of mystery and uncertainty. Each time I was pregnant, waiting for baby to come was an exercise in cultivating patience. I was also invited to deepen in the capacity to trust, and to stay rooted in the present moment.

Readiness for birth wasn't confined to having the diapers stacked and the baby clothes washed. At the end of each pregnancy, all the things on my to-do list were checked off. I then entered the period of simply waiting. I'd find myself asking, "Why wasn't baby coming?" And that's when I'd finally settle into the liminal space. Things began to look different. Time seemed to slow down. The dust was often kicked up. Routines were disrupted. There were new things to consider. Perhaps each baby knew there was yet work to be done, and not the nesting kind—but rather the existential kind.

The Waiting

Rowan was born five days after his due date, which I could reasonably handle. But my second son, Braeden, had kept my husband Chris and I in suspense for what seemed like an eternity. The due date was May 12th and it was now edging on May 24th. Why was he taking so long to be born? Every day felt like the slow passing of a lifetime. I was ready to burst and my emotions were running amuck. My midwife suggested we focus on any unfinished business in our relationship or family lines. Was there something that baby wanted us to resolve?

Chris and I considered any cobwebs that needed to be cleared. All of the sudden, the seeming weeks of eternity transformed into daily revelations about self and past. Buried memories resurfaced. Birth stories were told and re-told. We turned over our own family experiences, considering our own experiences of being first-born and second-born. We felt ourselves in a long line of emotional and genetic ancestral patterning, generational knots to be untied or left alone.

Then came the questions: *What do we want to do differently this time? What patterns do we need to shift? What growth is required of us in order to foster peace, health, sanity and love?* We considered our own preparedness to parent. *Are we really ready? What does ready mean?* The waiting offered a lull in the rush of routine, a brief dip into a valley where we could climb up a bit to see the big picture of our lifetimes from new vantage points.

The Birth Terrors

It was also while in this liminal space of reflection and waiting that I experienced what I call my "birth terrors." I had just been through several nights where I was awake and restless at the 4 o'clock pre-dawn hour. I was cranky, irritable, profoundly restless, agitated, and frustrated. I chalked it up to exhaustion as I thrashed my way back to sleep. But during one 4am wake up, I was ushered directly into the unexpected jaws of panic—a literal cold sweat, shortness of breath, and vice clamp around my chest. My body was shaking and I suddenly felt with clarity how much fear I had yet to metabolize about birth. Perhaps this was one of the unresolved threads that needed to be experienced before my son would be born?

All of this utterly blindsided me. Out of nowhere, and yet obviously hiding in the deep crevices of my body, lived the cellular memory from my first birth. All over again, I felt the residual fear from my first birth when Rowan had been in my birth canal for those four long hours. I had been pushing as hard as I could without seeming to move him even a fraction of an inch. It struck me that I too had been "stuck" for several hours in my own mother's birth canal. During the weeks of waiting at the end of my pregnancy with Braeden, I'd called my mother and asked her to tell me my birth story again. She had been pushing as hard as she could after an exhausting 40 plus hours of labor. She'd ended up on her back with me inching my way down, my skull compressing her tailbone. It had been a long, slow labor for her as well. I, too, had lingered in the birth canal.

All of this passed through my awareness as I panicked at 4am. What if I got stuck again? What if I couldn't get the baby out? Intense claustrophobia propelled me to run to the open window in search of space. I tripped outside at 4:50am thinking "why don't people tell you all this is wound up in birth? Why don't more people talk about these things?" I did laps around my neighborhood block, crescent moon shining overhead. The early morning singing of the birds called me away from my worries as I caught my breath.

Until this moment, I hadn't known any of this lived in me. Instead, these forces of emotion and cellular memory went underground until they were triggered again, looking for release. I remembered tidbits from my yoga practice, and from my training certificate in sensorimotor psychotherapy. A voice was trying to speak through the chaos: "All you have to do is just feel your way through this. You feel what you are letting go of." Feeling was a path to metabolizing some of what I was experiencing in my body. I could burn this up and clear the way for a new experience. Would this cellular memory and experience of *stuckness* serve me? Yes, if I feel into it again, difficult and unsettling as it was, and move through it.

21

Sorting Out Old Karma as Preparation

There are so many emotional, physical, and psychological edges women bump up against and move through around birth and pregnancy. Do we fully acknowledge the vast spectrum of emotions that can emerge? Do we talk enough about it? For me, all of the sudden I was in it, past it, forgetting the intensity of it—until I walked into an unexpected pocket of remembrance.

Ultimately, I was sorting out old karma in preparation for a new life. Meanwhile, my husband Chris was realizing that he had work to do around having been the second-born son, just as Braeden was our second-born son. The time of liminality reminded us to reflect on the unique and precious human life that we were about to welcome, along with our own intricate weavings of story and history. This was the gift of waiting. Birth impending. Pregnant. Attending to the spaces in-between. Full of meaning, if we are available to it.

Each time, I was humbled by what it took to bring new life onto this Earth. For a brief moment in time, a pregnant woman holds the sublime reminder of a passageway between worlds. She is the circle of yin and yang holding a small universe of life inside. The invitation is to learn to bask in the not-knowing and to trust forces at work beyond our control. Only then, resting in the liminal realm of mystery, can we enter into free-flowing unbridled creative synergy: that which truly does propel forth new life and make the world go 'round.

The Invitation

There are often emotional, physical and psychological edges we bump up against and move through around birth and pregnancy.

Consider whether this is (or was) true for you.

What is your own birth story? Revisit it.

Are there lessons that want to emerge?

Consider how you work with periods of mystery or uncertainty.

What positive approaches have worked for you in the past? What new approaches might you embrace?

Birth

Birth splits you open like a seed,

sending shoots in a thousand molecular directions.

All of the sudden,

everything is different.

Bones shift,

inside becomes outside

and a new shape takes root...

Each of my births was intense and beautiful in its own way. I gave birth to my three boys at home - all within a span of five years. My longest labor was with Rowan, who was born in the summer after 21 hours of laboring. Braeden arrived in the full swing of spring right after a torrential rain storm, finally landing in my arms just before the end of my 42nd week of pregnancy. My third son, Kienan, came in the heart of winter, after only three short hours of active labor.

A common thread that ran through each birth was the intensity of the experience. There were vast emotional swings—excitement, happiness, apprehension, exhaustion and wonder—and sometimes the feelings seemed to occur all at once. Each time I gave birth, I waited for nature's forces to invite me to open into something I could only distantly imagine.

Birth of Kienan

With Kienan, I had just gotten well enough after a bout of illness to be on my feet again when the early signs of labor set in. I cleaned the house, took a walk, made dinner, and called my mom to give her the signal to drive from Wyoming to be with our family for the birth. She arrived just before dinner and helped with Rowan's and Braeden's bedtime. I rolled into active labor at 7:25 pm with back-to-back contractions, dipping into a timeless realm of touch and go pain and blurred vision. I was doubled over in discomfort now, and I found myself calling out for help.

I tried to practice surrendering into each contraction. I heard myself bemoaning "I hate this!" I had not been one to love being in labor. I resisted it fiercely and with each birth had a difficult time relaxing at any point in the process. Modesty slowly went out the window. The midwives arrived and I was fully in the dance of dilation. I marveled that this part of labor wasn't about "contracting" but rather expanding - and I tried to meditate on the beauty of the star-gazer lilies I'd bought for this moment.

"All you have to do is float," said my midwife as I struggled. She was trying to help me go with the flow, reminding me that I didn't have to exert intense effort for this part of the birthing process. But for me there was no effortless opening, only the shaky handing over of myself to one moment and then the next. There was only the raw practice of trusting a process greater than myself.

I moved into a warm bathtub for relief. I finally felt the urge to push. Had it been one hour or five? I had no idea. I knew that my mother was resting with my older boys, and I knew that I didn't want to be alone. I also knew that I no longer cared about words. The truth was now unhinged and uncensored. My husband Chris told me to "stay with it" - encouraging me to stay with the intensity of the experience and breathe through it. I remember hearing myself say, "I have no choice but to stay with it!" There was no getting out. No escaping. No distraction. I heard my yoga teacher's voice in my mind as a fuzzy line of background noise: "The only way out is in." *The only way out is in.*

Making the "Impossible" Happen

Labor and birth is a time when the rawness of physical pain and discomfort can push us into surrendering to a force greater than ourselves. With each birth I was at times terrified, although I didn't know why. I had to pass through a gauntlet of taking responsibility for overcoming exhaustion and doubt. The moment required that I muster my deepest strength and willfulness to push my baby down and out. My midwives had said, "All you have to do is trust that your body was made for this." *And*, when it was time to push, I couldn't just sit there idly waiting either. At the very least, the moment required presence. At the least, the moment required a square confrontation with the reality of what was arising, particularly when the reality was uncomfortable, painful or exhausting.

With Kienan's birth, the exhaustion was accompanied by one wave of pressure after another. I had no idea where to go or how even to move with a head like a bowling ball two centimeters away from crowning. All I knew was I had to get him out. I was dripping sweat and standing next to my bed, my two arms stretched out across my mattress looking for support. I was seeing stars and begging for rest, even though I knew that the final moment of reckoning was upon me like a pressure cooker.

This was when I had to dig deep and find a reservoir of strength that I'd only tapped into twice before with my other births: *a woman's gritty willfulness to make something happen that feels impossible.* For me, this was no easy birth. It was raw, uncomfortable and painful. There was no bliss, no rest, and certainly no peaceful hypnobirthing place to relax into. For me, birth was a series of deep, wild screams of disbelief coupled with absolute, unfiltered awe. How the hell does all this work? How the hell do women do it? So normal, no big deal—and so literally transfiguring at the same time.

And then he was out—blue, sticky body on my chest, loud cries—and the midwife comforted both of us by saying, "You only have to do this part once." And in that moment I felt again my own birth—squeezing into life through a narrow passage, "contracting" into form. At the same time I felt my death, which perhaps will take me into the opposite realm of expansion. I felt back to the burst of my waters breaking earlier—a crackling preparation for baby's entrance—and I wondered if somehow we come via darkness and water into this crazy world of light and go too from this world into a different light?

All this passed through me as we welcomed my youngest son—and yet all that really mattered now was the skin touching skin, and the awe-filled reminder that being in this body is a blessing unlike any other. Sensation! Touch! Love! Pain and pleasure blurred into one of the most glorious moments of grace: a mixture of relief, contentment, sharp pains, aching muscles, sore jaw and forehead, and stinging base of body. How hard it can be, and yet somehow the difficulty blends with the heart-wrenching love and gratitude, quiet moments of awe unfolding into a new life.

The Invitation

Recall moments in your motherhood journey when you have had to dig deep to draw upon your reservoirs of strength.

What lessons did you gain from those experiences?

Consider the yoga teacher's injunction that "the only way out is in."

What does this mean to you in your own life?

Does it hold true for you? If so, when and why?

The Other Side: Paying Homage to Life

"Making the decision to have a child—it's momentous. It is to decide forever to have your heart go walking outside your body."

~ Elizabeth Stone, Author

The moments after birth: I call it "being on the other side." Giving birth is one of those moments in life when there is a clear before and after—the continuum of life as it is known is profoundly interrupted. There is a giant pause in the experience of time's passage. Priorities shift. A new normal slowly emerges that can't fully be imagined before baby arrives. There is the anticipation, the waiting and wondering, the anxious uncertainly (for many) about labor's when and how... And then, suddenly, you are on the other side. Birth happens. Baby is here. A mystery in the form of a new child has come into the light. And despite our wishes for time to stop just for a moment, life moves on.

Savoring

In those precious moments resting with my newborns, I was invited to savor and acknowledge life's great transitional moments. Something dramatic had happened. A new life had come into the world and we are forever changed by it. For these days and weeks immediately following baby's arrival, we can be steeped in a slow wonderment. Life is centered around this tiny being, and yet at the same time, there is the largeness of a full lifetime perspective. Memories of my own childhood flashed. Family stories came to the fore. My mother told me again of my own birth. I felt the presence of old friends. I looked at my children and wondered about their future.

When greeting each of my children, it was like falling in love all over again. When I was pregnant with Rowan, I'd come across Elizabeth Stone's quote about the decision to have a child being momentous —and it was. With a little one in my arms, I could understand the notion that to have a child *"is to decide forever to have your heart go walking outside your body."*

Each time I gave birth to my sons, I wished for time to stop. The pace of life outside of the small world of nesting with a newborn could sweep me up in a fast flow. I could easily forget the importance of slowing down. I wanted to greet each transition with intention—and tend to my life and family with appreciation. I wanted to slow down to steep myself in awe and gratitude at the passage of time and the blessings bestowed. So how could I mark this time as sacred? *Savor.* Acknowledge life's great transitions.

Lying In

My midwives encouraged me each time I gave birth to stay in bed with the baby for several weeks. "Don't even walk up or down the stairs for three weeks.

Don't pick up your other children. Just rest." Each time I struggled with heeding this advice. While wanting to pause and rest, I also wanted to jump back into the energy of my life. I wanted to see friends, get outside and generally "get things done." And yet I knew that this phase of being with my newborns did indeed go by fast. I didn't want to rush it. I also knew that having the option to "lie in" for several weeks was a gift. Not all mothers can swing it. For some, work demands or other responsibilities make this practice not possible.

I decided to go with my midwife's advice and to "lie in" with my babies. It felt very counter-cultural in a world that seems to value how fast a mother can rebound and get back to Pilates or the grocery store. "Lying in" was an invitation to stay in bed with my baby for an extended period to rest, recover and bond. Even if it wasn't a full three weeks, I was close —taking as long as possible to stay horizontal, getting to know my little ones.

Those weeks are full of sweet memories. I would gaze at my children and reel in their preciousness. I would relish the cuddling and the sweetness of their tiny features and soft touch. I knew the moment would not come again. I seized the rest and time for connecting.

The experience of lying in with my babies gave me the opportunity to mark a threshold for both myself as well as the whole family. Crossing from one side to another in any life transition offers the opportunity to pause, reflect and wonder. Lying in was the perfect way to pay homage to what had been while also gracefully entering into the newness of what was becoming. Most importantly, I could slow down and pay homage to life itself as I snuggled with my new little soul.

The Invitation

*Often we can be in a hurry to get
from one thing to another.*

*Consider how you can slow down
to savor time with your child.*

*Consider the transitions in your life,
both small and large.*

Take time to pause, reflect and wonder.

Walking the Labyrinth of Change

"A labyrinth is a symbolic journey ..."

~ Rebecca Solnit, Author
Wanderlust: A History of Walking

As my little ones grew, I danced the dance of surrender into the days of motherhood. The "aha" moments began to slow down, making way for a steadier rhythm of more predictability. It felt like a slow apprenticeship of descent and return—much like the walking journey in and out of a labyrinth. A whole cycle of transformation was coming to completion, waxing and waning like the moon cycles spread out into years.

After the arrival of each of my children, I'd eventually move a bit beyond the diaper years. At that point, I would take a quiet moment to register being on "the other side" of a massive transition. Unpredictability had ushered in more evenness. Lessons had begun to coalesce. I've settled in, I suddenly realized. It felt like skin sinking into sand on a beach after a long period of being away from familiar shores.

Suddenly there was space to see the labyrinth journey into motherhood from the outside—to gain a perspective different from the center. There is being in the fire so to speak (which pregnancy, birth and early motherhood often feels like)—and there's a bird's-eye view of where one has just been. I am forever changed having traversed the leap from "maiden" to mother in the progression of life's generational dance. How we come out of transition into something new is just as important as simply marking the transition itself.

Transition from "Maiden" to Mother

Even years into the motherhood journey, I still find myself working through the transition. As a way to grapple with the changes afoot, I often reflected on a woman's journey from "maiden" to mother. The maiden phase of a woman's life, the time before we are mothers, marks the springtime of life, like the budding of a new flower. It is a time of youth, vitality, activity, and adventure. The focus can be primarily inward. As a mother, our attention is now called outwards. It is a time for care-giving and responsibility, where the focus necessarily rests on our children, our families, our homes and communities. It is an entirely new phase of life, with deepened responsibility.

When I crossed the threshold into becoming a mother, my whole experience of "self" shifted. Gone were the mornings of sleeping in according to my own schedule. Gone too were the uninterrupted moments of musings or wanderings. It was all different now that I had a constant companion by my side. I was no longer a woman alone going about my business in the world. I was a woman with children.

Many of the changes were welcome shifts in my days. I loved the quiet moments sitting next to a sleeping child, admiring small toes or a colic in the hair. I loved the physical closeness, the silliness and the giggles. I loved experiencing the world through the eyes of my little ones—trying to imagine what it was like to discover new things.

As I settled in, the questions began to unravel. *What is this next unfolding? How can I integrate the lessons of becoming a parent into a next iteration on life's path? What do I need to let go of from the last phase as I enter this new one?* So many times I had heard parents say, "Where did the time go? My child is eighteen now and I don't know where those years went." Eighteen months or 18 years—I wanted to mark the moments of change as sacred.

As mothers, how can we make life's moments of transition marked, sacred, and noteworthy? Like a short (or long) carpet rolled out for ourselves, we can mark our transition into a new chapter with intention. The key is: *Do we pay attention?* My whole life was changing and I wanted to pause in order to take note.

Pregnancy, birth and the spaces in-between had taken me on a profound crash course on letting go of one phase in order to fully enter another. I'd wrestled with letting go of the body I'd known before childbirth. I'd come to welcome a new "me" in the mirror—and she was now wearing the likes of nursing pads and maternity pants. As I traveled farther into the metaphorical labyrinth, I'd been prompted to hand over my ego and "self" to larger forces of creation and chaos beyond my control. Now was the time to trust that each life transition would continue to teach me the art of letting go and letting be what simply is.

Lessons along the Path

I chose to approach my years of having children as a journey—and the image of the labyrinth resonated. Each time I'd walked a labyrinth, I'd been given the insight I needed at that time. It offered me some comfort that there was a journey in—and a journey out. No matter what I was experiencing, it was part of a larger path.

The labyrinth had also taught me to tune into the present moment, no matter where I was. The transitions I was going through could at times be disorienting, even while accompanied by peaks of joy. As I twisted and turned deeper into my own experience of motherhood, the questions I was asking shifted. *How could I live more fully and passionately in this new chapter? How could I integrate lessons learned into being the most compassionate mother or person? How could I stay grounded and centered, even as I felt like a new person emerging from what felt like a rite of passage?*

Just like light somehow splits open a seed, I made myself available to insights in my daily actions, trusting that glimpses would emerge as guides along my path. Like a rock in water, I'd thrown myself into this stream of my life's path, and now I had to simply trust the tides as they did their work. With awe, I could marvel at time's smoothing gestures of slow transformation.

The Invitation

When you became a mother, did your experience of "self" shift? If so, how?

What is different now? Consider how you have transformed.

What lessons have you learned?

PART II

What to Become Now?

A Whole New Normal While Tending Hearth & Home

"I wonder: instead of pining for the way it was, what if I accept the way it is? This strikes me as both the most obvious thing in the world and the most profound."

~ Ann Kidd Taylor
Traveling with Pomegranates: A Mother-Daughter Story

Becoming a mother unfurls us into a new phase of life, often beckoning many of us to wonder, "What to become now?" It's a time of grappling with a new normal - where the work required multiplies and where patience is tested in new and intense ways.

In the early years of motherhood, I often found myself yearning for what was, even while simultaneously embracing the many new joys. The motherhood journey was akin to a marathon, with the endurance test feeling never-ending at times - especially when sleep was scant.

The laundry piled up along with the dishes. I was home more than I'd ever been. The orbit of my life seemed to have shrunk. I was struck by the way in which motherhood and its subsequent responsibilities prodded me to contemplate escape routes. I was faced with a choice: lose myself to the endless task lists or settle into this new experience with a sense of freedom and fulfillment. I began to embrace the idea of dwelling contentedly at the proverbial hearth of my home.

In Part II, I reflect on my own process of welcoming the newness that the motherhood journey ushers in. I share my path of embracing acceptance in light of challenge and change. The next series of invitations were revealed - and they all had to do with uncovering a non-discriminatory state of mind and heart, where gratitude and love can dominate the landscape of duty and responsibility.

What to Become Now?

"Did we trust that here, in this place, we would become the most beautiful version of ourselves?"

~ Christiane Pelmas, Author of *Women's Wisdom*

Giving birth often speeds up the reflection process around letting go of the past, transitioning more fully into a new phase of life and motherhood, and entering the doorway to a new stage of life. It is time to let go of yearning for what was, while more fully welcoming the newness of what is now.

For me, the period of years when I had my babies felt like a gateway to an entirely new period in my life. My personal story was solidifying. The children that I had only dreamed about when younger have been born. The lines on the face have become a mainstay. I often found myself looking at my children with wonder at the passage of time—one foot planted in the summer of youth, the other foot lifted and moving in slow motion to a new realm of a lifetime. The transition into motherhood often gave me pause, and I found myself asking more and more often, *"What to become now?"*

Rediscovering Ourselves in New Contexts

As I mused on this question, the glimpses that emerged were about the simultaneous loss of what I used to relax into while also stepping into a new, more fluid identity: *a re-birth into mystery*. It was a period of loosening and non-knowing. Just like what is true of the winter seedlings turning toward the light of spring, a seed in darkness doesn't know yet what the light will bring. And still we can choose to root ever deeper to place, to let go of past attachments, to face squarely any emergent resistances to change, and ultimately to surrender to a complete transformation.

In *The Middle Passage,* author James Hollis says that "the realistic thinking of midlife has as its necessary goal the righting of a balance, the restoration of the person to a humble but dignified relationship to the universe." While not all mothers of young children are necessarily in "midlife," the image of a "middle passage" resonated with my own journey of entering into family life. It was an entirely new path with new responsibilities and daily rhythms. As Hollis went on to write in his book, many entering a "middle passage" are moved to ask, "What work, then, needs to be done now?"

This question felt intimately connected to my underlying inquiry of "what to become now?" As a mother, my life purpose had shifted—and not only in the broader sense. I often felt submerged in the five rounds of daily dish-washing, or the constant cleaning up of messes or the piles of clothes to be washed. The work of caregiving and homemaking was no small thing, and when balancing that with work outside the home, along with relationships and self-care, it felt impossible some days. Nonetheless, I chose consciously to pay attention to what work needed to be done—both the practical work as well as the work that was personal, spiritual and existential in nature.

I often found myself reflecting about my own mother during this time—and how at different times in our lives, women are invited into a liminal space of rediscovering ourselves in new contexts. She too, in her 70s, was asking similar questions to mine. She and my father live just a few hours north in the sweeping open spaces of Wyoming. For six years my mother was a dedicated caretaker of my grandmother LaRue, who was born in Chicago in 1916 and lived to be 100 years old. During one of my visits while she was immersed in caring for my grandmother, Mom said to me that her guiding question was *"Who am I now?"* She was standing in the doorway of her 70s. Together, we were tending the hearth of our homes and caring for both younger and older generations: attending to the full spectrum of life. She was tending to my grandmother, the realm of life's end all too near. I was tending to my three small children, taking their literal first steps in life. We both were tasked with continually rediscovering ourselves as we swam in new and liminal phases of our lifetimes, holding the pieces together for life's continual beginnings and endings.

Staying Dedicated to the Important Questions

What work needs to be done now? And who am I now? These seemed good and solid guiding questions as I settled into motherhood and a new passage of my life story. There was the care-giving, the tending, the keeping of hearth, yes. But also, there was the process of becoming (and already being), a spontaneous and clear expression of the creative, shifting energy of the feminine form. There was the work of staying dedicated to the important questions in life: *How are we living and loving? What imprints are we making on this precious world? How are we embodying a humble yet dignified relationship within the order of life? How does our spirituality manifest? As my yoga teacher would often ask, "What is the texture of our conversation with the Divine?"*

As I journeyed further into motherhood, I reflected on my own experience of spirituality. I had James Hollis' words in mind about the middle passage of life and how to cultivate "a humble but dignified relationship to the universe." I began to ask myself how my experiences with spirituality could inform how I was parenting. And how could spiritual teachings shed light on the difficult spaces encountered in the daily reality of raising children and tending hearth?

I had grown up Lutheran, my father a Lutheran pastor who had planted the seeds of the importance of open-mindedness, right action, compassion and service. In college I spent several of my spring breaks going on a pilgrimage to Taize, an ecumenical monastery nestled in the rolling hills of southern France. It was at Taize that I first encountered a more contemplative and mystical expression of Christianity. After college I joined the Peace Corps in Mali, West Africa, living in a small village where Islam was the primary faith. I then attended Naropa University, a Buddhist-inspired university in Boulder, Colorado, where I learned about and began practicing mindfulness and meditation rooted in the Tibetan Buddhist tradition.

Over the past 20 years I found myself over and over again at retreat centers and monasteries in Europe, India and the US, deepening in my own commitment to spiritual practice and understanding. I began to identify with the mystical aspects of all the great religions, seeing the common threads throughout. I wanted to practice bringing an experience of the Divine into all of my moments, regardless of what I was doing or where I was.

Motherhood as a Spiritual Practice?

In the transition to becoming a mother, I often felt that the lessons emerging were similar to the central lessons of many of the great spiritual traditions that I had encountered. In grappling with what I was becoming, it seemed the perfect time to apply the wisdom of the spiritual masters. Furthermore, wasn't this the perfect opportunity to delve into this experience of birth and motherhood for what it was—unique to women? What spiritual lessons were to be found here, in this uniquely feminine realm of experience? Here I was in a great life transition, trying new things and being tested in new ways each day. Motherhood was showing itself as viable and relevant a spiritual practice and path as any other. There was no room for separation here. I couldn't remove myself from being a mother. It was now a constant self-identity and an ever-present relationship.

The word religion means to be bound to a path (from the Latin *religiare*)—and the root word of 'yoga' comes from '*yuj*,' to be yoked (as in yoked to a path or yoked to the Divine). As a mother I was now solidly bound to this new path. I was struck by how often daily responsibilities (and particularly the responsibility of parenthood) were perceptually and culturally divorced from the realm of 'spiritual practice.' And yet one perspective I had encountered was that ultimately spiritual practice is at its root the practice of *your most revered state*. It didn't matter if I was in a monastery or on a meditation cushion. What mattered was how I was living and who I was becoming, even in the moments when toddlers were crowding underfoot while I was trying to cook dinner. What work, then, needed to be done now? What was my most revered state, and how could I practice being that, particularly with my children?

Practice: Even in Ordinary Moments

I was being invited to step into the realm of my inner world in order to clarify what my most revered states were—and what I most wanted to embody in this lifetime. The next step then was to rise to this calling through literal 'practice' throughout the 'ordinary' moments of rest and responsibility in any given day. After all my spiritual seeking and soul-searching, this—right here with the diapers and the wet wipes— was the path of embodiment and authenticity, when I could truly live and breathe my values and my love. My family was always right there, inviting me to be my best self at each moment. I was slowly beginning to understand that there was no separation between 'life' and spiritual "practice." I could begin to walk into my days and relationships with more presence, more seamless awareness, and a more clarified expression of what I most wanted to be radiating through my presence.

Too often motherhood responsibilities are taken too lightly or undervalued. Also, too often are the unique insights of women and mothers dismissed. I resonated with Sarah Menkedick, author of *Homing Instinct: Early Motherhood on a Midwestern Farm.*

She had written an op-ed for *The Los Angeles Times* on why writing on motherhood isn't taken seriously. "Birth is a matter of blood and sweat and gore and suffering, of life and death... except: Only women can give birth," she wrote. So why don't people take writing about motherhood seriously? *"Because women do it,"* she reflected.

I was flummoxed by the ways in which motherhood duties seemed relegated to the realm of the mundane. What about mothers' stories and wisdom? What about how day in and day out we were tested? What about all the ways in which the "ordinary, mundane" moments actually pointed to so many of life's greatest lessons? Of course I understood that it didn't help that I often felt frazzled, unorganized, not "put together." I was always the one picking up crumbs, wiping messes, leading a pack of unruly kids. Nonetheless, I could also glimpse the truly regal responsibility that is raising and caring for another human being. It meant choosing to do the hard work required: to show up fully in any given moment, to come back again and again to my best intentions, and to embrace humility in the face of life's greatest moments of challenge and testing.

I chose to heed motherhood's invitation to stay focused on the important questions in my life. What was I becoming? What work needed to be done now? How could the experience of motherhood help me grow and evolve? As writer Christiane Pelmas (author of *Women's Wisdom*) says:

> *Perhaps now is when we allow ourselves to answer to something much greater, like the final question—did we lead relevant lives as fierce lovers and servants of this world? Did we hone our skills as love*

makers, body and soul, in this lifetime, finding an ever-bolder beautifully unapologetic expression of our gratitude and longing? And did we trust that here, in this place, we would become the most beautiful version of ourselves?

And then it struck me. Indeed, there is nothing else to become other than this: the most beautiful version of ourselves.

The Invitation

Practice letting go of yearning for what was, while more fully welcoming the newness of what is, now.

Consider what the most beautiful version of yourself is, or what your most revered state is.

How can you bring these parts of yourself more into your daily life?

Choose at least one thing to practice this week.

What work needs to be done now in your life?

A Whole New Normal

"The only way to make sense out of change is to plunge into it, move with it, and join the dance."

~ Alan Watts,
Author of *The Way of Zen*

Raising young children brings with it the widest spectrum of experience and emotion. There are the highs and sweet joys. Then there are the challenges, riding on the heels of some of the most poignant moments of connection and love. I often felt the motherhood journey was akin to a marathon, with the endurance test feeling never-ending at times. Just when I thought I'd crossed a hurdle, mastered a lesson, or entered the realm of sleeping through the night again, I was thrown a curve ball. Instead of catching it head on, I often tried to duck the ball with an internal dialogue of "no...really...this can't be happening again!" Chris and I made a habit of laughing as we imitated being stuck in a boxing ring with punches thrown. Like a comedy of errors we flung through our days, pans clanking, dishwasher running, laundry resembling a mountain, hours spent tending what needed tending.

The juggling was mind-boggling. I remember one summer day when I was carrying the stroller down the stairs from our apartment. Rowan was a toddler and had missed a step. I somehow managed to catch him while he was falling head first, even while holding the stroller in my other arm. That same week there was the moment when the full grocery cart careened towards the car and off the curb, and I somehow grabbed it before it crashed and sent food flying. Each time I'd been trying to balance keeping a little one safe while also just going about the business of an ordinary day. These are truly small wonders, and I've seen so many other parents participating in their own small daily wonders as well.

A whole world of appreciation has opened now that I am on the motherhood journey. How did I never notice it before? I've taken to marveling that any parent can somehow hobble through a day with any degree of sanity, patience and grace with young children in tow. The other balls to juggle don't stop flying at us either, and meanwhile we have to be sure our children aren't running into the street or flinging all the boxes of cereal bars off the shelves. When caring for another human being, life simply becomes a more defined mélange of joys and hardships, the peaks and valleys of a day so unpredictable that I am forever alert and on my toes.

A Balancing Act

Identifying the abundance of my life was essential during those days of chasing and juggling. I often heard myself lamenting about being tired, or feeling pressed for time. It often felt like there was always something else to be done. The required vigilance took its toll. I often reflected on how doing the balancing act of parenting and working can create the conditions for a scarcity outlook. Seeing life from this perspective, it's easy to think: *"There isn't enough time! There's no food in the house! There is no time to clean! There is no time for exercise! What about me? There is no time for self-care..."*

Without being mindful of these tendencies, suddenly five years can pass and we've missed soaking in the treasures of this phase of life. We can root ourselves in scarcity mentality and let this be our compass (which only bogs us down), or we can count our blessings over and over again and look around with fresh eyes. Yes, some things have to go on the back burner: like sanity as I knew it before, like a pain-free back, a finished conversation with a friend, a slow cup of tea in the mornings, or an easy trip to the grocery store. And so it is! Make way for a beautiful kicking newborn, the adventure of a toddler turning the living room into an obstacle course, and ultimately *a whole new "normal!"*

It can be a slow process of letting go into what is. On most days I tried to integrate down time and quiet time into my time with the kids. During an attempted moment of yoga, my oldest son Rowan crashed a plastic tow truck into my foot. He often reminded me to not take myself too seriously. Yes, my needs matter, but there was also something to be said for the etching away of my attachments to "rest," "exercise," "alone time" and all the other things I was pining for outside of the realm of my motherhood responsibilities. It isn't that these things aren't important or shouldn't be a priority in their own right. But now there is the opportunity to discern what is *most important* and work to make time for those things. In the balancing act, we have to give up certain things. We get to try out what it is like to live without some of the things we thought we couldn't do without (like sleep, for one!).

The result? *Parenting can make us more malleable, more flexible, and less bent on attachments to particular outcomes.* After becoming a parent, things pass through me differently. At times I've interpreted it as aging, heaviness, a weight of continual responsibility. There were times when the air alone seemed to offer resistance for me to work through. Other times I feel I'm being set free into an unchartered territory of lightness. In this experience, my body, along with my patience, thresholds and norms, are stretched, pulled and worked on. The result is I feel my unavoidable, liberating, eventual transformation into something new and unimaginable.

The wonder of a "new normal" was indeed upon me. Turning a brilliant corner, I could choose to set myself free into the profound rite of passage journey that children offer up. With screws coming loose, a new doorway opens and a marvelous view prevails.

The Invitation

Parenting can make us more malleable, more flexible, and less bent on attachments to particular outcomes.

Are there areas of your life where you could become more flexible?

Consider your current attachments. Where might you be holding on too tightly?

Whatever phase of life you are in, consider a "new normal." Name at least three things you are grateful for.

As if your screws were indeed coming loose, opening a new doorway, what new view in life wants to prevail?

Tending the Hearth

*"The symbol of Goddess gives us permission. She
teaches us to embrace the holiness of every
natural, ordinary, sensual dying moment."*

~ Sue Monk Kidd,
The Dance of the Dissident Daughter

Some days, the "new normal" of parenthood left me
feeling cloistered. During a phase when I felt
particularly tethered to my home and hearth, I
decided to read Sue Monk Kidd's *Traveling with
Pomegranates: A Mother-Daughter Story*. It was the
perfect book to aid me in contemplating the marvel of
sacred journeys. It's a lovely tale of Kidd's
adventures with her daughter who is just discovering
her calling in life. It's also an exploration into the
phases of a woman's life. The story follows their
personal experiences during travels in Greece,
France and Turkey. It also explores the mythology
and lore surrounding images of ancient goddesses of
antiquity that they encounter along the way.

The book helped me to remember my own past as a
traveler and adventurer. At one time I was fancy-free
and footloose, gallivanting around the globe on world
adventures. I was always plotting my next escapade.
At 19 I'd chosen Niger, West Africa as my locale of
choice for a study abroad program. There I'd worked
at the National Hospital and taken a bus tour across
Niger, Burkina Faso and Mali with 15 other students.
Over the years, I'd backpacked solo across Europe,
done a Buddhist Vipassana retreat in Dharamsala,
India after two short stints on organic farms, and

had lived in a Senufo village of 600 people for two years in southern Mali. When I was home in the US, I was an avid lover of high altitude hiking and road trips to see friends. You could say that being at home with babies provided quite a contrast.

And Now...Tend the Kitchen

New mothers receive, often unexpectedly and without adequate preparation, the profound and often inescapable invitation to tend the Proverbial Hearth. I'm not sure what I thought would happen when I made the leap to becoming a mother, but I don't think I was prepared to tend the fireside kitchen in the way it required. Part of me thought I would be able to do it all: keep my sense of fancy-free, have one foot in my career as an environmental non-profit program director, and keep up with friends while also somehow being a present and loving mother (with a clean house, to boot).

I often struggled to balance my fierce desire for independence and autonomy with the draw of motherhood which entailed homemaking and tending to the needs of my kids. How many of us resonate with Sue Monk Kidd when she writes that she'd imagined herself "traveling more in the orbits of goddesses like Artemis and Athena, whose forms of the feminine are about the search for an independent self?" She writes:

> They (Artemis and Athena) are the ones who could bring home the bacon and fry it up in the pan. I haven't pictured myself as a "mother goddess" type. My children have always existed at the deepest center

of me, right there in the heart/hearth, but I have struggled with the powerful demands of motherhood, chafing sometimes at the way they pulled me away from my separate life, not knowing how to balance them with my unwieldy need for solitude and creative expression.

In seeming contrast there is the ancient Greek Goddess Hestia, the Goddess of the Hearth or Fireside, whose task is to keep the home fires burning—symbolizing nurturing and the continuity of a spiritual flame within the home. As I delved into her history, I was surprised to find that she, like the free-wheeling Artemis and Athena, was the sort of goddess who is self-contained, independent, and un-partnered. She lived in her own circle of dominion.

Hestia did not have a traditional 'emblem' like other goddesses. Her practical divinity was perhaps too obvious and self-explanatory for such grand measures. She also was not known to have the grand adventures that other goddesses often had. (After all, according to ancient lore, she didn't even leave the Hearth for the sacred processions of Gods and Goddesses). Instead, the divine feminine face of Hestia ultimately points to the ability to dwell firmly and contentedly in one's place without need of fanfare or external recognition. She points with grace to the ability to belong to one's home as a gesture of radical settling into the nurturing role of sitting fireside, at the helm of family life.

Finding Home

My life as a mother felt like such a contrast from the seeker's heart and the Goddess archetype that flies the expanses of sky and earth: the woman who journeys, who goes on pilgrimages, who ventures into the unknown, who controls the forces of nature and the vicissitudes of harvests through her ebbs and flows. I recognized the tension in my own experience as I settled into home more often—still pulled to far-away places and drawn to the lures of adventure and movement. I was still resisting what I'd labeled the "specter of routine." Yet with the surrender into the rhythm of routine also emerged the deepened settling into place, the ability to actualize *dwelling* in the best possible sense.

Before becoming a mother, I had not been one who was archetypally drawn to home and hearth. And yet, I could see the roots present in my longing to tell the story of where I come from through my family history, the valuing of good food and shared meals, and the contentment of creating beautiful, intentional space. Hestia had never called me with her quiet, subtle expression of creative power - and yet she is the one who makes the world go round so to speak. She, tender of fire, hearth and family, maintains order and feeds life. She is the backdrop of rhythm in the flow of life. She is there to bookmark 'home,'—that which we return to and that which is our ground.

Traveling with Pomegranates had reminded me that of course there is a time for pilgrimage - a time when a physical journey can support the marking of a transition or transformation. Perhaps a great lesson of motherhood is the awakening into realization that journeys can indeed also be profoundly inward into vast regions of the fire of heart and soul. We can also journey to the realm of hearth and home, family and food—where nourishment comes in the form of simple, quiet meals and slow walks up the stairs with sleeping child in arm. Hestia knows the art of doing each mundane task with great love and as a gift, with no need for recognition or fan-fare. And still, it is she who keeps the fire of life burning.

It was now time for me too to keep the fire of life burning in my own small orbit of home. My children were calling me to the hearth in ways I could never have imagined. Climbing up on a stool next to the kitchen counter, Braeden would often lend his little hands to baking projects. For one of Chris's birthdays, Rowan decided he wanted to make a homemade pie. It was time to roll out the dough, get out the broom, and then cuddle on the couch with my little ones and a good book. Indeed, the story of Hestia reminded me to dwell contentedly at home— relishing in the simple forms of nourishment that tending hearth offers: quiet moments with family, shared meals, and the possibility of doing each task with great love.

The Invitation

Hestia invites us to dwell firmly and contentedly in one's place without need of fanfare or external recognition.

This week, practice more deeply settling into your home and 'hearth.'

Consider what inner journeys you have ventured on since becoming a mother.

What are some of the simple joys you have found in tending hearth? Take time to notice and perhaps journal about your experience.

Laundry, Dishes, Liberation?

"And yet, I cannot help but look around some days and wonder: As a daughter of the feminist movement, was this the endgame? Am I living the dream that they held in their hearts?"

~ Devon Corbet,
Author of *Zen and the Art of Housekeeping Blog*

I often felt tethered to the home during the early years of parenting. Much of that time at home offered a much-needed respite from the outside world, where I could let my children settle into free play and unstructured time. While at home I did a lot of laundry, served a lot of snacks and meals, ushered forth multiple daily naps with singing and shushing, and sat on the floor rolling balls and building blocks.
It's no wonder many mothers feel stir-crazy after a previous life of comings and goings as we please.
Now we are pulled to home like waves pulled to shore. Everything we've lived before often seems distant and impossible.

Devon Corbet, a fellow mother and friend, had been sharing her own reflections on motherhood and tending home in her *Zen and the Art of Housekeeping* blog. She often wrote on the rhythm of housework and the ever-present tasks of homemaking. One of her posts got me thinking about my own experience of what it means to be a daughter of the feminist movement. The long days at home, parenting and home-keeping, could be hard. The sense of responsibility was ever-present. My kids seemed to have some three to four needs each minute, my baby needed to be held and fed. There were poop-filled diapers to be changed every hour, or so it seemed. The messes piled up. I often tripped over the toys strewn about the floor.

I'd been working part-time for an environmental non-profit since my first son was born and some days going to work did indeed feel easier. I could self-regulate with ease at work. I could get a drink of water right when I needed one. I could choose to be my introverted self for a spell. Parenting young children and trying to maintain a sane order at home alternately tossed me into a cocktail of extroverted, non-stop output, where multitasking was a survival skill.

What about "Liberation"?

Devon's reflections on housework, feminism and women's liberation got me thinking about what "liberation" means in the context of homemaking and childrearing. I'd just given birth to my third son, Kienan, and I'd been home. Really *home*. In the three weeks since he was born, I had ridden in a car only once. Since he caught a cold at four days old, we received few visitors and avoided all public places. On warm enough days, I took neighborhood walks with him in a baby sling.

During the early stretches of parenting little ones and tending the family hearth, I found myself swinging on a trapeze amongst varied emotions. There was the trapped feeling, the wanting to "get out"—both literally and figuratively. Then there was the calm bliss of sitting quietly with my new babe. There was the complete overwhelm of looking around and seeing nothing but work that needed to be done. Then there were the sweet moments doing a craft together or giggling about a silly story. Some moments, there was the wishing for something other than what was presently arising. Other moments, there was a sweet surrender into the present moment, accompanied by a peaceful appreciation of my children. The truth was that the trapeze swung, nonetheless. There was the bliss followed by frustration. There was irritation. Acceptance. Love. Gratitude. It all happened, sometimes in a span of ten minutes or less.

I was struck by the way in which motherhood and tending hearth prodded me to contemplate escape routes. There were times when I could lose myself to the ceaseless task lists. There were other times when I was invited to settle into an experience of utter freedom and fulfillment. There were times when I felt overwhelmed by the responsibility of caring for my children. There were other times when I wanted nothing else.

Devon had prompted me to contemplate the endgame of the feminist movement—and while I didn't know what that ultimately was, I did know that there was a new and different kind of "freedom" to be found in the motherhood journey. I did now know that as a woman I am given a profound opportunity to maintain a peaceful, sane order of my home. I know that there is an ever-present risk of losing myself to mere execution of tasks. I also know that sweeping doesn't have to be just sweeping; it can be akin to cleaning the temple. The quality of attention we bring to what we do is essential.

If Seeking Something Else, I Was Not Free

If I saw the tasks associated with being a householder and parent as "separate" from my deeper passions and yearnings, then I would lose an opportunity to find "freedom" in the orbit of my home life. Ultimately, I wanted *everything* that I was doing with my time to be a full expression of myself. This seemed to offer a critical insight about "freedom" or "liberation."

If I was always seeking something else, I was most certainly not free. If I assumed one expression of myself was "better" or more desirable than another, I would miss out on a seamless experience of non-discriminating contentment. This meant if I gave more weight to my professional work over laundry, or my yoga practice over a dish-washing practice, or a solo hike at 13,000 feet over a neighborhood stroll to the playground, I was missing an invitation to find freedom and fulfillment in my day to day life. If I alternately gave myself over fully to what was asked of me in the realm of parenting and homemaking (even though cultural forces and even personal preference might deem it less alluring), I could enter the free and clear realm of non-grasping and non-seeking mind.

My years of interest in spirituality were coming to the fore and serving me in ways I could have never imagined. I remembered the Sanskrit word "moksha," which points to freedom, letting go, releasing, and liberating. In both Hinduism and Buddhism, moksha points to freedom from the cycle of life and death, while also connoting self-realization. The notion of moksha reminded me to "let go" into the present moment, whatever it demands or offers. It reminded me to simultaneously release expectations of how I think something should be, especially if it looks different than what is presently true.

While there will always be social conditions requiring liberation movements, there is also always the possibility of an internal orientation of liberation, in the spiritual sense. Regardless of externals, we can bring a free attention to everything we do. For me, that meant that I could choose to rest in the center of acceptance, which is ultimately a great expression of day-to-day freedom. I could choose to embody a wild love that fuels an experience of expansiveness and liberation, even in the seemingly small orbit of nuclear family and home.

The Invitation

If you're always seeking something else, you are not free.

Consider the times when you may assume one expression of yourself is "better" or more desirable than another (professional work over laundry or a yoga practice over a dish-washing practice).

What would a seamless experience of contentment look like in your life?

Practice shifting the quality of attention you bring to your everyday tasks this week.

When Equanimity Is Rearranged

*"Equanimity is the hallmark of spirituality.
It is neither chasing nor avoiding but just
being in the middle."*

~ Amit Ray,
Author, *Meditation: Insights and Inspirations*

Some spiritual masters say that equanimity is the true mark of spiritual maturity. Equanimity is a steadiness of mind and presence, even under stress. Since my children were born, I'd lost my sense of equanimity more often than I ever have in all the years of my life. I knew what it was about: finding and encountering the unpracticed, undiscovered territories in myself that didn't yet possess strength in the face of challenge. In this way, my children—and motherhood—had become my greatest life teachers, offering up opportunities day in and day out to exercise my faculties and emotional reserves in new and unchartered ways.

No Problem!

I was someone who had always gotten feedback about being patient and calm. As I headed in motherhood, I smugly thought I'd mastered equanimity. I thought I could handle whatever was thrown at me. I thought I'd surely burned up life's imbalances through self-awareness, study and dedication to spiritual practice. And then I dove off a cliff into parenting and lost my traditional reserves. I was utterly disoriented. Everything felt rearranged. It was a whole other layer of rediscovering a new "normal." How was I supposed to do all the things that were required of me while also holding on to any sense of equanimity or patience? The experience was incredibly humbling.

In my scramble to find the wisdom I needed, I attended a book group focused on conscious parenting. A fellow parent spoke on how when parents are well rested and prioritizing self-care "the intuition is intact, patience is intact, and the love impulse is intact." But how could I maintain a steady life pace when balancing the needs of my three young children? Sleep, exercise, spiritual practice, connecting with others, the joy of an uninterrupted creative process or even an uninterrupted conversation had suddenly felt like luxuries. My ability to be patient was not as intact as it used to be when self-regulation and self-care could happen on my own terms.

During the early years of parenting, I often found myself in an unchartered space, grasping for sanity and centeredness when I needed it more than ever. I was pressed for sleep. My sons seemed to know just how to nudge me towards my edges. At first I didn't know how to resolve conflicts or what my philosophies were in relation to everything from schooling to discipline to diet. The learning curve felt steep. Just when I needed balance, equanimity and those resources of self-care the most, it seemed they were taken, gone, and seemingly unavailable—just like the genie disappearing back into a bottle.

As parents, the baseline of physical well-being through rest, community support and an overall sense of health and vitality shifts, and yet the demand to function and show up at our best doesn't relent. In fact, it is only amplified. For me, the invitation was to serve my children and others through finding a new baseline of balanced surrender into what is. Instead of engaging life from a place of struggle or stress, I could choose to respond in a relaxed way with a non-problematic disposition. Instead of emotionally responding to difficult moments from a place of exhausted reactivity, I could reset with a deep breath and answer the tug at shirt or throw of egg across the room with a relaxed, non-problematic disposition. *No problem!* After all, young children respond to our state so much more than our words.

Re-framing What Balance Is

I scrambled to find a new ground of balance. I wanted to embody equanimity under my new circumstances—maintaining composure and a sense of peace even during times of stress. I began to practice slowing down as a first gesture of adapting to the changes underway. I made a point to take time to feel whatever I was feeling. I noticed that even just naming my exhaustion or frustration could itself be nourishing. It felt like a first step in recapturing a sense of balance during times of stress.

Smaller gestures of self-care like a cup of tea or a brief hot shower became more poignant. I decided to engage the present moment with a re-frame of what an experience of equanimity was or could be in my life. It looked different now and that was okay. How could I juggle all that needed juggling? All I knew is that I would do one thing at a time. I would try to relax more and crave 'other' less.

At times the flurry of activity made it more difficult to pay attention to my own needs. I knew that I would never find equanimity that way—so I made a point of checking in with myself in the in-between moments during my days. *Had I eaten enough? Did I pack water for myself? Was I breathing deeply or shallowly?* For me, the slowing down to check in with myself pointed the way towards the elusive realm of equanimity: that mark of spiritual maturity. I could catch my breath and regain my composure. I could tune in to the simple joys of being with my boys.

Life had changed dramatically. Composure and evenness of mind had at times eluded me. Yet like an archer aiming to hit its mark, I considered Amit Ray's reflection on equanimity: "It is neither chasing nor avoiding but just being in the middle." I realized I could do this. I could rest in the middle of whatever was happening—finding my own simple way, even when my sense of balance had been rearranged.

The Invitation

Equanimity is the ability to maintain composure and a sense of peace even at times of stress. Consider what this word means as it relates to your life.

Identify ways in which you can cultivate equanimity in your family and in how you respond to situations.

Instead of engaging life from a place of struggle, practice responding in a relaxed way with a non-problematic disposition.

This week, find ways to relax more and crave 'other' less.

Living Fully, Being Happy

"Each thought, each action in the sunlight of awareness becomes sacred...I must confess it takes me a bit longer to do the dishes, but I live fully in every moment, and I am happy."

~ *Thich Nhat Hanh,*
Buddhist Monk, Author and Peace Activist

Life had been rearranged in so many ways. Slowly I'd settled into a new era. I'd become a mother of three young boys, and while life was full and there were challenging moments, I was in love with my children. Each day, my boys tugged at my heartstrings. There were unexpected surprises, daily moments of silliness, and new adventures to be had.

When I became a mother, I had no idea I would become well-versed in dinosaurs or construction vehicles. My boys drew me in new directions and I happily followed. We spent afternoons at the creek, tossing rocks and following the tracks of bugs. We took family field trips to see dinosaur bones and tracks. I learned how to make home-made play dough. For many years, my boys loved waking before dawn, so I discovered the loveliness of early mornings while the stars were still twinkling. A comforting rhythm of new routines unfolded, ushering in a new experience of life.

A new "normal" had indeed set in, and I was happy. I'd become more focused on home life and more steeped in responsibility. But I'd also kept my sense of adventure. Yes, I made the breakfast and school lunches, went to work, changed the diapers, mitigated sibling conflicts, played Legos on the floor, cleaned the kitchen, invented a new bedtime story each night—and then *voila*, I woke up and did it all again! It was practical life at its fullest—but it was also fun.

I noticed that being mindful of how I was approaching each day helped me to find contentment in the new rhythms. As Thich Nhat Hanh had reminded me, "Each thought, each action in the sunlight of awareness becomes sacred." I didn't want the practical demands of my days to eclipse my enjoyment of life. I didn't want a year (or ten) to pass by without me drinking in the joys—even when cleaning up messes, making beds, drawing the daily bath water, or wiping the counters. I could just wash the dishes, and be happy. I could sit on the couch and read books with my kids, and be happy. I could spread the sunlight of my awareness onto and throughout my days, and be happy.

I often reminded myself to "be in relationship with the present moment." This was something my yoga teacher had shared, and it resonated. What did this mean? It meant that it didn't matter what I accomplished in any given day, but more *how* I was relating to what I was doing. What did matter was to *be merely present with what is*. Every ordinary interaction in a day—whether it was with dishwashing soap, the garbage can or my precious sons—could be experienced as part of an ever-present holy portal, beckoning my full-bodied entry. It was always there as an invitation—inviting me to settle in, slow down, and take time to fully enjoy my little ones.

Mindfulness

Jon Kabat-Zinn is a mindfulness meditation teacher, author and founder of the Mindfulness-Based Stress Reduction Program at University of Massachusetts. He defines mindfulness as "paying attention in a particular way: on purpose, in the present moment, and nonjudgmentally." It is a quality of attention that can be brought to each moment and situation.

While a student at Naropa University, I'd been lucky to have received mindfulness and meditation training. At the time, I had imagined that I'd use these skills in my broader work in the world. I'd been studying Environmental Leadership, and mindfulness practice had helped me to stay present with discouraging realities facing our planet. Yet it also ushered me into the ability to just stay present with whatever came up—whether it was nervousness, conflict, uncertainty or difficulty.

My professors taught me to pay attention to how I was breathing and how my thoughts were unfolding. They pointed me to noticing how I felt, physically. I was learning the skills to listen more deeply—to others as well as myself. These were life skills that I'd find myself drawing from well into the future. They were straightforward lessons, all rooted in the importance of staying present.

As I swam farther into the sea of parenting, I found mindfulness practice to be an essential ballast. I didn't want to let the sweet joys of these early years pass me by. Mindfulness was a way for me to practice paying full attention to each moment, even if it was flying by at the same fast-forward pace of my children's quick footsteps. As with a meditation practice, I could observe what was arising, take it in, and move into the next moment. Just like watching clouds passing in the sky, I could also simultaneously observe my thoughts and reactions. During the moments when I was steeped in multitasking, I could choose to come back to focusing on each inhale and exhale. This grounded me again and again in the tangible experience of my present moment. Breathing in, breathing out.

Learning to be more fully present allowed me to ride the waves of transition and change during early motherhood. It was an ongoing practice. It was the invitation that continued to beckon. As I settled into my "new normal," I could pay attention in a particular way. I could choose to be purposeful. I could root myself in the present moment. When it was all too easy to judge myself or my children, I could practice being non-judgmental.

Finally, I could live fully and happily in the practical, logistical realm of life, while also being sure to soak in the treasures that my boys were handing me every day. I could take time to delight in simple tasks and moments. I could relish in the humor and wonder of hours in the company of young ones. I could remember simple enjoyment, and gratitude could then reign in the new landscape of familial duty.

The Invitation

Practice paying close attention to what is arising, both internally and externally, in any given moment.

As Jon Kabat-Zinn suggests, try to pay attention non-judgmentally.

Rather than be consumed with the practical demands of life, practice enjoyment of the simple moments and tasks.

Make a list of the things you are grateful for.

PART III

The Dance of Too Much

"The path of motherhood has a beginning, but no end. It's constantly changing and constantly challenging. Along the way, we encounter our personal limits over and over. We fall in love over and over...

On this path of discovery, as on any spiritual path, our pretensions are shattered, our minds are blown, and our hearts are opened."

~ Susan Piver,
Author and Meditation Instructor

Motherhood brought with it an invitation to practice balance in the midst of juggling. In a culture that prides itself on "busyness," I had for a long time prioritized a "slow and steady" approach. Above all I wanted balance in my life. But now living in balance was more complex as I navigated parenthood along with work, other relationships, and managing my home. The early years of parenting often prodded me into new realms of responsibility, where I truly greeted the limits of my strength. I often felt inadequate in the face of what was required.

The practice of yoga became a stream of refuge in which to immerse myself when the going got tough. I realized that I was too often doing the dance of too much - and that if I didn't pay attention, I was at risk of "going through the motions" carelessly. I decided to slow down, reassess what was most important, and take time to notice where I was unnecessarily depleting my reserves. I made nourishment a practice. I discovered that with less and less room to "get it all done," there was more and more space for humility.

In Part III, I explore how we as mothers need periods of time when there is less doing, more being, less carrying and juggling - and more resting and stillness. Ultimately, I was working to balance the forces of being and doing. Indeed, when rest is available, we can bask in it - and when a lovely moment is upon us, we can take note.

Instead of Pushing Too Hard, Open

"Yoga does not just change the way we see things, it transforms the person who sees."

~ B.K.S. Iyengar,
Yoga Teacher, Author and Founder of Iyengar Yoga

When I was 25 years old, I decided to give Hatha Yoga to myself as a birthday present. I was living in Chicago at the time, and there was a studio in my neighborhood that I always walked by on my way home from work. I started going to classes and never stopped, later becoming a yoga teacher and lover of all forms of yoga. Of course becoming a mother made getting out to classes as well as teaching more difficult. But the practice has stayed with me, particularly during more chaotic times.

Paying Attention

There were many physical demands during pregnancy, childbirth, breastfeeding and early motherhood. As someone who had been immersed in a body-based practice, I wanted to pay attention to the shifts underway. I could feel the possibility of getting stuck in new patterns, especially if I was shuffling unaware between tasks. I was often carrying one of my boys on a hip—or schlepping strollers and heavy car seats.

The practice of yoga had become a vehicle through which I could open myself to fresh revelations about my life. I could shed light on and within my own experience. Certain yoga poses had the capacity to usher me down a rabbit hole into deeper layers about the truth of my experience. It was during one of these practice moments that I realized a simple truth: many moments of my motherhood journey had been rooted in *pushing too hard, rather than opening.*

Feminine Strength?

It often happens in a physical practice: the impulse to muscularly will, physically push oneself to the "other side"—even when what is ultimately needed is to slow down or back off. (Think: running too long or hard when you've been sick. Think: lifting too much weight in order to keep up with the person next to you. Think: doing a difficult Pilates practice at two weeks postpartum). I'd witnessed a lot of women (and myself) pushing through something simply for the sake of "getting things done" or "getting to the next place." When I realized that I too was doing this, it struck me like a light bulb turned on in a place I'd never been. Sometimes this kind of pushing ourselves to a next level *is* strength, and sometimes it is definitely not.

At this point, I was a mother just figuring out how to relate to doing the dance of too much. I wanted to figure out what strength looked like here in this new place. In all the newness, I'd too often erred on the side of over-extension. As a result, I was sick more often and tired more often. My body's aches and pains piled up. Some days in the flurry of caregiving and homemaking, I forgot to eat well. This seemed to me to be an all-too-common pattern for women. Was it a superhero complex? Was it because so many women were just good at multitasking and over-extending? But what was the cost of doing too much?

I didn't lose sight of this question as I paddled my way through busy times. I knew there was no strength in whittling myself away into an exhausted collapse. There was no strength in moving through life like a strong energizer bunny if I was moving mindlessly. Instead I wanted to pay attention to what each moment required, and then decide how to do the dance of responding without compromising myself. It was a lesson I had to learn over and over again.

When I pushed myself too hard, I was losing connection to vital threads of my own inner wisdom. Beyond always being "busy," "tired"—or making a habit of "pushing through" in order to meet one more obligation—I wanted to exchange a different kind of energy in the world. How could I be more open to listening to myself and my body? How could I move through my life with a sense of flow and mindfulness, rather than self-induced pressure to do more or be more?

Living steeped in this awareness pointed to a different kind of strength, and ultimately a feminine sort of strength. It felt rooted more in the heart realm and less in the will and intellect realms. Instead of doing too much too fast, the invitation was to give outward from a place of relaxation. These were times when things had to get done and someone had to do it—and the key was to live each breath of the doing while tuning in to my deepest places of knowing. I had to ask myself again and again: What is personally right in this moment? Then I could glimpse more of my true nature, slowly becoming clearer and less fettered—and more capable of the profound love that the awakened force of motherhood entails.

The Invitation

How are you already strong in your life?

Where does your strength come from?

Consider what it might look like to 'open' rather than 'push' in your life.

Choose 3-5 moments each day and practice being available to any wisdom or insight that wants to come through.

The Lesson of the Downward Facing Dog

"We can be sure that the greatest hope for maintaining equilibrium in the face of any situation rests within ourselves."

~ Francis J. Braceland,
Psychiatrist and Educator

For over a decade, I'd been blessed to work with the Northwest Earth Institute. This amazing non-profit organization promotes sustainable lifestyle and voluntary simplicity. Before I had children, I worked full-time in the Portland, Oregon office, overlooking downtown from the eighth floor. On a clear day I could see Mount Hood, its snowy, pointed peak calling me to the wilderness. I had always been a lover of nature and was blessed to find an organization working to educate and inspire people to take better care of our planet.

After the birth of my first son, I was able to reduce my work hours to part-time and began working remotely from my new home in Boulder, Colorado. I'd wanted to be closer to my parents in Wyoming and my brother who lived in Boulder. He and I had moved to Colorado years prior to go to graduate school together, and I missed him sorely. I made the drive from Oregon to Colorado with a U-Haul when I was four months pregnant. I remember feeling like my whole life was ahead of me, and the open road brought with it a sense of excitement and anticipation for the new chapter ahead.

Little did I know that even with a part-time work schedule, I would still feel as if I had jumped off a cliff onto a conveyor belt of new challenges of work-life balance. Switching gears between parenting and my professional life became a juggling act full of humor and complexity. I remember the first conference I presented at when Rowan was just three months old. I was leading a workshop on Voluntary Simplicity only later realizing that I'd been leaking breastmilk, standing in front of the group with fresh stains on my shirt. (I'd missed the memo about wearing those pads.)

Even working part-time, there were periods when more was demanded of me. When Rowan had just turned two, I'd been in charge of organizing a biannual national conference. There were many moments when I didn't know how on earth I would pull it off. Rowan still hadn't slept through the night and I was perennially exhausted. It was the intense drain of what I called an "over-responsibility" period.

Balancing What's Required?

During this particular period, my roles as mother and professional came to a head as I stood metaphorically on a balance beam, juggling 50 balls. For a year I'd been heading up the conference planning efforts (which translated into an eight-page, single spaced to-do list). Rowan was sick and needing more from me than usual, and I was up in the middle of the night worrying about things such as the projector carts, name tags, and adapter cords. I dove off a slide into the tumult of 15 hour workdays and a long weekend of tireless execution. I rode the wave of work until I crashed.

How did mothers do it? I wondered. *What about those mothers who work full-time? What about the single mothers?* I was flabbergasted that anyone could do this balancing act. I was stretched to the edges of what felt possible to sustain. I got sick and felt more exhausted than ever. Even though I somehow pulled off what needed to be done, recovery was slow. I couldn't seem to bounce back the way I had before. I wondered whether recovery was the essential yearning after which I should be pining.

Even though my stress levels were at a new high and my health was at a low, I began to consider how to live reasonably in a period when more was demanded of me than I was used to. So my question became: *How does one recover?* How on earth do mothers balance all that is demanded and keep going, especially when breaks feel few and far between?

Enter the Downward Facing Dog

The question pointed me to the proverbial downward facing dog pose in yoga: the pose that burns when you hold it for long periods of time. There is of course the choice of coming out with humility and intention —bowing out and bowing to our limits. But there is also the choice and possibility of conducting a different energy of strength and structure, staying in the pose because it is required of you. There is the choice of staying with it because you have no choice but to hold certain elements together in life, and you may as well do it while breathing deeply and lengthening your spine.

Holding the downward facing dog is a lesson in endurance and personal sustainability. Over time, I aimed to find and know well my limits while maintaining a sense of balance based on that self-understanding. I often go too far and tend to forget my deeper self-care, testing those boundaries. The same pattern was mirrored in my personal and professional life. I had stretched myself so far as to land into the place of nursing my second cold in a month. I'd been trying to balance the work and motherhood conundrum, and realized that for now it was a path with seemingly no reprieve.

So I remembered the lesson of the Downward Dog. Gulping for air doesn't serve longevity. Deep, slow, sustained breath does. Letting certain parts of one's bodily system crash in exhaustion doesn't serve the integrity and full-functioning of the whole. Maintaining awareness of the full body working in flow, even when tired, serves to foster a sense of cohesion and personal structure around which and from which many things are possible. An open heart and spine go a long way in facing life's challenges with grace and composure. And feeling one's hands and feet rooted into the ground provides a needed stability beyond oneself when one's personal experience becomes harried.

Finding Rest in Exertion

The trick for me became doing more than I ever thought possible while also finding rest in the midst of the discomfort and exertion (such as burning muscles in a really long-held yoga pose). Just like that second wind during a long jog, in moments of resourcefulness I could draw from a mysterious reserve of love and purpose. I found I could tap into this reserve when the rubber hit the road and there didn't seem to be a brake pedal.

I remember the moments after that initial work conference. It had been in Port Townsend, Washington, at the northeast corner of the Olympic Peninsula. The conference had gone well and the work was temporarily complete. Rowan and Chris had joined me on the trip but were staying off-site. There was a light rain falling, and I was so excited to switch gears more fully into family life again. As I fell asleep next to Rowan that night, I felt his little hand on my arm.

In the silence, I reflected on the lesson of this time of juggling. The invitation was this: *when there is no stopping, let go and surrender to the ride.* There is nothing to change, nothing to resist. In yoga, we say, "ride the wave of sensation!" Yearnings for rest may be ever-present, and that too will come one moment —with a mysterious return to quiet, a pause of hanging in the balance between being and doing. For now, exertion calls, but so too does riding that calling with a slow breath of acceptance and peace.

The Invitation

When stretched to the edges of what feels possible to sustain, remember to take deep, slow sustained breaths.

This is what serves longevity and endurance.

Consider your own relationship to exertion and recovery.

Do you tend to over-extend until you crash?

Identify ways you can weave in rest, even when you are in the middle of an 'over-responsibility' period.

When Greeting the Limits of Strength

"24/7: once you sign on to be a mother, that's the only shift they offer."

~ Jodi Picoult,
Author of *My Sister's Keeper*

During my third pregnancy and immediately following my third son's birth, I was dabbling in a complete physical breakdown and burnout. There was the cough, the flu, the stomach bug, the sinus infection, the strep throat, the month of antibiotics. Then there was the rib pain and shortness of breath. Was this just a nervous breakdown or was motherhood actually driving me to my edge? It turns out the rib pain was either stress-induced (an acupuncturist's conjecture) or a pulled muscle (a doctor's conjecture). Whatever the cause, the culmination of so many repeated illnesses and physical rarities showed me the absolute limits of my strength.

A trip to the doctor was like a visit with a prophet. "No—I'm not worried at all," she said. This was even after I had listed the above maladies and she checked my ribs. "I see this type of immune system lapse and extreme stress all the time with mothers of three or more children... Some years are just harder than others."

24-Hour Needs Cycle

Now don't get me wrong. I'm sharing some of the more challenging moments of my motherhood journey because it was often in these moments that the greatest insights shone through. The day-to-day life was still blessing me with all sorts of joys and simple pleasures. I was still enjoying the wonders of being pregnant and parenting my young boys, even while also not feeling my best. I remember the drive to preschool in those days. There was a farm with baby horses along the way—and we would stop to greet them almost every day. There were hugs. There were cuddles. Life rolled along and I with it. But this third pregnancy—did it have lessons for me!

When I'd visited the doctor in hopes of some relief, I couldn't believe she had told me what I was experiencing was absolutely normal for a mother in America. *What? This was normal?* I pondered over and over again how I got to this place of breakdown and burnout. I took it upon myself to conduct experiments about whether the 24-hour needs cycle of young children was really true. In 10 minute blocks, I began tracking needs, requests and necessary safety interventions. First of all, the exercise helped to infuse some humor into the situation. Secondly, it indeed did confirm that burnout is perhaps a predictable response when you are responding on average to five to nine needs and interventions in any ten minute period!

There was the crying for milk. There were the diapers full of poop. "More nuts!" "Water!" "Help!" There was the head bonk with tears followed by the toy yanked from a hand by the older sibling, then a smack on the head from the toddler to said older sibling. The needs were all perfectly normal and reasonable -

usually pertaining to water, food, sleep, bodily functions, needing help, comforting a fall or mitigating a conflict. What amazed me was that the needs cycle lasted all day long!

Slow Down & Make Nourishment a Practice

So, yes, some years were harder than others. And, yes, this particular period of motherhood was actually showing me the limits of my strength. But beyond rounds of antibiotics, doctor visits and trips to the acupuncturist, how to cope? It was indeed a period of soul-searching. I'd been sick for five months and something had to give. I took to my journal to try to sort out what direction I needed to take.

First, I decided to tackle my experience of feeling spread in a million directions as well as moving too fast. I focused on slowing down the whole orientation. This was primarily an internal gesture and required taking my time responding to everything that was arising in any given moment. When I slowed down my orientation, it shed light on what I could do with more ease. Where was I unnecessarily depleting my reserves? How could I move and speak in ways that reflected parenting from a calm, resourced place? I made that my goal.

Second, I took stock of how little time I was making to really take care of myself. I decided to make nourishment a practice. This meant drinking enough water, eating good foods, and getting enough sleep. It also meant lighting a candle nightly for a period of time, becoming best friends with a heating pad on my neck, and making time for exercise. The key here was *making* time. We can make time for *what is important*—and self-care has to be on the list. The invitation became to relish in the smaller gestures of nourishment in a day. Relish drinking water. Make sure to drink enough of it. Relish the two minutes of lying down. Take time washing your face. Eat slowly.

Tending to All Emotions

These practices did make a difference. I let myself just be open to what was constantly arising with my children—and that was enough. Spending time with them was nourishing as well—especially when I could see beyond the 24-hour needs cycle!

As a mother of young kids, I often felt a pressure for everything to be rosy. I desperately wanted to only focus on the tiny blessings and sweet moments of connection in my days. I wanted to relish in the shared art and cooking projects. I wanted to be one of those women who was crafty and creative, home-cooking every meal and serving it up with a kid-friendly twist. But as I contemplated these desires I also felt that the shadow side of motherhood wasn't being addressed. I felt like my culture had created a Hallmark, cookie-cutter cliché of what motherhood should look like, and it involved blowing dandelions into the wind and looking at the clouds in wonder and amazement while everyone partook in familial harmony. While I caught glimpses of these precious moments, the truth was that the stressors of pregnancy and motherhood were also making me profoundly unwell.

I wanted to be honest about all the emotions I'd experienced during the months of being sick. I'd been trending towards depression and depletion, and it felt important to acknowledge this dimension of mothering along with the brighter sides. During this period, I set out not to over-identify with any given emotion or feeling. Yes, as the doctor had said—some days, weeks and years could be harder than others. I could just let each emotion be true, but not only identify with the ill health or difficulty. So I rested in the perspective of observer or witness. I could experience this chapter of motherhood for what it was: a chapter. I could also experience the contentment, the curiosity, the wonder. Motherhood encompassed it all.

Motherhood was always inviting me into fresh experiences and perspectives. Wait a moment and things would change! Just as clouds slowly change shape overhead, the experience of motherhood was also like shapeshifting. There was the joy, and right there with it, I was greeting a limit of my strength. A true gift was how I'd been invited into an entirely new range of emotions. There were highs and lows—and together they formed a glorious edge upon which I now walked.

The Invitation

Slow down. Take time to notice where you might be unnecessarily depleting your reserves.

This week, make nourishment a practice.

Consider: How can you make room for all of the emotions entailed in your motherhood journey?

Journal about, or draw, key elements of your experience.

The Dance of Familial Chaos

"Dance then wherever you may be..."

~ Sydney Carter, Lord of the Dance

As someone who had historically self-identified as a perfectionist, having to let some things slide since becoming a mother has been humbling. I often feel inadequate in the face of meeting my three boys with as much presence and attention as I would like. I feel inadequate when I make mac and cheese for dinner for the 100th time in a year—or when I yell when a dish breaks instead of responding with patience. It comes up when I fall short of my intentions, when I'm late consistently for play-dates or work, and when I can't seem to get through the laundry pile.

The word adequate is from the Latin, "*adaequatus,*" which means "equalized"—as in "to be equal to what is required." It turned out that parenting was showing me my own limitations at every turn. Daily I don't feel equal to what is required. I don't mean this in a self-deprecating way, I mean it practically. I can't respond to three requests at once. I can't do as much as I once did.

Freedom Beyond "Accomplishment"

Parenthood can feel like a constant fall on the face: a literal trip up the stairs. There is food on the wall (and pummeled into the floor). Work tasks take longer to check off. Phone calls go unanswered. Letters written three weeks ago are still not mailed. And then there is: *"Where are my keys?" "I swear that diaper was in my bag."* and *"Mom! Why didn't you wash my sweatshirt? You said you would!"*

With less and less room to 'get it all done,' the upside is that there is more and more space for humility. And with that emerges the invitation to dance in the freedom of just being yourself—regardless of and independent of what you are able to 'accomplish.' Ultimately, freedom arrives when I am just myself, moment to moment. Nothing more or less, just doing one thing at a time, calmly (or not) juggling all the balls thrown up in the air.

I'm reminded of Nataraja, the Hindu Lord of Dance, who is also an expression of the deity Shiva who dances a cosmic dance of bliss. He is most often depicted with one foot on the ground pointing to his embodiment, and the other foot lifted in the air, pointing to release or liberation. His dance is meant to release us from the illusion of separateness. Instead, we can realize our interconnectedness within a unified whole where we are not a separate "I" but rather embedded in a web of mutual cause and effect.

Nataraja reminds me that I too can be a dancer in the seamless, never-ending field of current familial chaos. I don't have to be thrown under the bus of overwhelm and the feeling of not measuring up. I don't have to worry so much about what I am or am not getting done. I can instead just do the Dance.

Dancing the Best We Can

I'm blessed with a group of fellow mother friends who I email and video chat with regularly. I call it my "cyber women's group." The women are my best friends from college—and over the years, we've shared the ups and downs of our family lives. Each of us does our familial dance in different parts of the world, and yet we always find common ground. A recurring theme is how we strive to bring balance to our lives.

During a particularly poignant email thread, we'd been connecting about the need to let go of our perfectionism. Maybe we couldn't do it all, after all. Maybe it was best to do our dance the best we can under the circumstances, and then let go. My friend Edwige summed it up perfectly. *"I looked at this beautiful baby next to me and I just said to myself, "Let go, just let go." And so I relinquished myself over to my life—and to not being able to control everything around me. I accepted that I cannot be perfectly rested any more, or perfectly prepared. I am a parent."*

I love this. Even when we are riding along the edges of overwhelm, exhaustion, or a feeling of 'not measuring up,' we can choose to let go of trying to control all of the outcomes. Instead we can dance our seamless, perfect dance within life's ongoing variables—meeting what comes with undivided attention and love.

The Invitation

*Remember, with less and less room to 'get it all done,'
there is more and more space for humility.*

*Practice letting go of trying to control
all of life's outcomes.*

*What would it look like in your life to dance a
seamless dance, even within familial chaos?*

Make a list of ideas.

*Meet whatever comes with undivided
attention and love.*

Weaving a Divine Thread

"I began to understand what bound Pearl to silkworms' simple mystery... In front of us, all around us, was the energy of life and growth."

~ Belinda Jeffrey, *One Long Thread*

My experience of motherhood has shifted many times over the years. There were periods when I didn't sleep much and I often asked myself, how far can I stretch before dissolving? I was up again, down again. Midnight. 2am. 5am. 5:30am. A day never ended. One day simply blurred into the next. There were periods when conflict kicked in and motherhood seemed to require a Ph.D. in Conflict Resolution and Peace Studies. Some seasons required more of me at work. Other seasons required more of me at home.

But easefulness also reigned—and the struggles that marked many periods in the first few years began to fade. There were slow summers when we could scrap the busy schedule, sleep in, and wear our pajamas until noon. There were new games invented between brothers that stretched their imaginations. Some days I could indeed sit back and relax.

Had I worn out the lessons of those earlier phases? There was the swinging between being and doing and how to be present in all the moments in-between. There was the search to find a way to do the dance of "too much" with as much grace as possible. And there was the desire to soak up the lessons of the era and integrate them for a lifetime of living well.

The Silkworm

During some moments of my motherhood journey, I'd indeed felt worn down and worn out. Perhaps there is no coincidence as to why we say "worn down" along with "worn out." All of the sudden we've worn an experience down to the point that the wearing has served its purpose of growth. But like a stone thrown about in water, we can't see our edges being smoothed while we're in the crucible of change.

I took time to pause and reflect on the massive shifts that had taken place in my life. I was now in my late 30s and with three boys in tow. The silkworm came to mind, with her ceaseless work. She only pauses to rest a handful of times before she spins the cocoon that will hold her while going through metamorphosis. She spins with little rest until ready for her transformation.

Meanwhile, out of steady effort, one of the lightest, most beautiful substances is born. Like a new cloak of understanding that is ultimately translucent, light, free-flowing like silk—I too was wearing a new understanding of parenthood. This was an understanding that transmuted difficult periods into a loving lightness of being when the parent-child relationship has struck its balance, found a flow. The work doesn't stop, but the weaving goes on. And sometimes we simply aren't able to see the beauty of the weaving until a moment of noticing is upon us.

The Experience of Beauty

Indian philosopher and writer Jiddu Krishnamurti says, "For most of us, beauty is in something, in a building, in a cloud, in the shape of a tree, in a beautiful face." He asks whether beauty is "out there," or is it rather a quality of mind that one brings to each situation? He says that "like joy, the understanding of beauty is essential." For me, the key to tapping into my contentment was to tune myself into an awareness of beauty, even during those periods when I felt like I was doing too much. I had to remind myself to continually pause to take stock of the beauty woven throughout my life.

The moments of pause invited me to find the inner lens that recognized beauty. I could then practice seeing through that lens, regardless of external circumstances. As Krishnamurti reminded me, the experience of beauty is a sensitivity born from gratitude, curiosity and awe. It is a quality of one's entire experience that can transcend the so-called "mundane." With this in mind, I could focus on the everyday moments where beauty would unfold. I could waste not a moment drinking in the sweet little hands eating juicy beets, the foggy wakeful moments in darkened rooms while holding your little one, the fleeting cuddles before the onset of a fiery independence, or the charming streaks of food on chubby cheeks.

Just Resting...

I learned that when rest was available, bask in it. When a lovely moment is upon us, take note—just like basking in the emerging light of the spring season, or wrapping yourself in the lightest, most beautiful silk scarf. Contentment ran deep when I trusted the weavings of a simple life: the ebbs and flows of waking, breakfast, playing outdoors with no agenda, quiet moments reading together, or looking out the window at the changing seasons. A nap. Lunch. Laundry. Dinner. Green beans and raspberries. There does not have to be anything more.

Then there comes a moment when you can just rest into the fullness of simply digesting your experience. That is the lesson of silkworms, hanging in the balance between seasons—digesting mulberry leaves, weaving a divine thread.

The Invitation

Take pause in the midst of busy routines. Notice the seasons of your life.

Tune yourself into an awareness of beauty.

Each day, practice finding gratitude for the little things.

When rest is available, bask in it, and when a lovely moment is upon you, take note.

PART IV

Working with Difficult Emotions

"Difficulties are like the ornaments of a good practitioner."

~ Dilgo Khyentse Rinpoche,
Tibetan Buddhist Scholar, Poet and Teacher

My children got a bit older and I became a more seasoned mother. Still, I found myself confronting the same lessons more than once. Some of them were uncomfortable and I wanted them to go away. Some of them became like friendly reminders - each one beckoning me to do another piece of my own inner work. Not only did my children bring me back to my own experiences growing up, but they also served to confront me with my own edges of personal growth. One thing I had to figure out was how to stay present with what was uncomfortable. I had to be willing to face myself continually, even when I didn't like what I was seeing.

I was treading into a painful facet of parenthood that is too often reserved for the shadows. What do we do when we are faced with our own raw edges of patience? What are the tools needed in order to work with the difficult emotions? What about the humbling doorway of mistake? And how do we, as mothers, express the energy of anger from a place of union, connection and integration?

Part IV tells the story of how I worked with the difficulties of letting myself and my family down, the experience of failing, and the uncomfortable moments of losing control. Through it all, family life had become a means by which I could learn some of the hardest lessons.

The commitment to staying connected and present with one another was the glue that often held it all together - especially in the difficult moments of disappointment, anger or frustration.

Doing Our Own Inner Work

"Who we are and how we engage with the world are much stronger predictors of how our children will do than what we know about parenting."

~ Brene Brown,
Daring Greatly: How the Courage to be Vulnerable Transforms the Way We Live, Love, Parent and Lead

My brother, Robert Lundin McNamara, is an author of several books, leadership development coach, and accomplished Zen teacher and monk. A few years back, I had the great honor of attending one of his workshops on the *Gate of Inadequacy*. With my mother Joan at my side, we unpacked multi-generational patterns in our family line and marveled at the power of intention to parent in different ways than we were parented. My mother had been the sort of parent people dream of having, and I was lucky enough to call my own.

As a parent, I often feel overwhelmed with the responsibility. *What if losing my cool serves up long-term damage? What if I'm not saying enough encouraging words? What if I nag too much?* Despite all my work to be the best mother I can be, I know I'm far from perfect. I worried often about this. I knew how much power I had to shape my children's experiences. I wanted to be as careful and positive as possible.

My brother's workshop reminded me about one of

the most important things I could do for myself and my children: inner work. As author Brene Brown wrote in *Daring Greatly: How the Courage to be Vulnerable Transforms the Way We Live, Love, Parent and Lead,* "Who we are and how we engage with the world are much stronger predictors of how our children will do than what we know about parenting." I could work with how I engaged the world. I could worry less about strategies and tactics —and concern myself more with my own responses and relationships.

So I made a commitment to delve inwards into my own life story, programming and patterning. Perhaps I could come to peace with all parts of myself—even the wounded, embittered, lacking in confidence, angry, shut down, or dissociated. These are the parts that translated directly into less patience or more sharpness with my children. These were the parts that live in us as shadows. These are the very realms of our experiences that most need integrating and tending in the spirit of breaking generational cycles at play. I wanted to burn through anything that didn't serve my greatest capacity to embody patience, acceptance and love. I strongly believed that through the practice of love - *feeling* it, living it, breathing it - all things could transform.

The Great Unearthing

As mothers, we are powerful beyond measure. The weight of that often hung over me. Especially with small children, our words matter immensely. Our actions matter even more. We can sow the seeds of confidence, self-respect, bravery and self-worth. Often unaware, we can also sow the seeds of shame or heartache. To the best of my ability, I wanted to deeply serve my children. How could I be most aware of what I was transmitting to them? When I made mistakes, how could I reconnect and repair? In choosing a path of self-reflection and introspection—and in choosing to do my own inner work—I hoped to find some answers.

Before becoming a mother, I'd endeavored to unearth all parts of myself. By this I mean that I wanted to know myself well. What motivated me? Why did I do the things I did? Why was I even led to this kind of introspection and self-understanding? Perhaps it was the long years away, living in a small West African village. I'd had more time then to journal and reflect, and being in a different culture had often inspired deep introspection. Or perhaps it was my study of philosophy in college. I'd been prompted to reflect on my values, ethics and ideals. What was "the good life"? Was I living it? Or perhaps it was my German Lutheran upbringing where I'd been taught to be conscientious—perhaps to a fault. Or was it my practice of yoga? So many facets of my life had urged me to dig deep.

One nugget of wisdom shone through. Along the way, perhaps through the Tibetan Buddhist practice of *loving-kindness*, I realized that I could direct a loving regard internally—even towards the parts of myself that I wasn't as comfortable with or didn't like as much. This meant taking the time to shed light over and over again on the mysteries of body, soul, personality and habit that made up my particular human form. It meant staying with what was difficult. It meant not turning away from anything—and not trying to suppress or ignore the more complex and uncomfortable parts of myself and my experience. Only then could I live more fully in a realm where I was absolutely okay with what just was.

There was something I often found remarkable about motherhood. It was how it forced me to confront the more edgy parts of my experience in ways that nothing had in the past. It felt like a great unearthing. Being tested in new ways invited me to either face my edginess or push it aside for another time. The new situations I was in with my children brought out different parts of myself. I wondered why certain behaviors triggered me. Each time I lost my patience or felt incapable of speaking kindly, I had a choice. I could ignore the potential personal insights —or I could return to the hard moments when I was ready to reflect and consider the lessons.

Facing the Edges, Shadows & Blind Spots

The bottom line was that I could *intentionally choose* to follow a path of inner work that ultimately transformed my own particular sharp edges, shadows and blind spots. I committed to face myself fully and squarely with as little judgment as possible. I also committed to not turning away from what was uncomfortable or less than desirable. It was difficult —but with some practice and dedication, I could do it.

You see, motherhood has been the most humbling experience of my life. I quickly realized that this journey required more tenacity than I could have imagined. I grappled with uncertainty. What was right action in relationship with each of my children? How could I live with myself when I'd yelled? Why did certain behaviors send me flying off the deep end? How could I be more aware of my own responses and reactions?

I kept returning to the need for self-reflection and inner work—and the importance of a loving sense of regard both for myself and my children. Slowly, I became more fully seated in an experience of love. This meant just being in Love! It meant being in love with my children, my partner, the leaves on trees, the color of sky and Earth, the changing seasons, my parents, the ground I walked on, and yes—even the more shadowy dimensions of my soul.

It meant practicing humility when things didn't go smoothly. With a commitment to inner work, I could take time to process and reflect—and then loop back around with my kids to check in. How did we all feel as a result of a conflict? What made us upset? Why did we respond the way we each did? What could we do differently next time? Most importantly, what had we each learned? And how would we bring those lessons into the rest of our lives?

The Invitation

Commit to a process of "inner work" or self-reflection and introspection.

Begin by staying present with what is uncomfortable in your experience.

Is there baggage from your past that needs tending?

Are there wounds from your own childhood that inform how you parent today?

Hold all parts of yourself with loving-kindness and positive regard.

If that is difficult, begin with small steps. Journal about your experience.

Wrestling with Shadows

"The beauty of motherhood is in the folds and creases of our lives, the grimaces and tantrums, the moments when we have to grit our teeth to get through, when we pound on windows and yell and scream and demand better of each other and ourselves."

~ Robyn Passante, Author & Journalist

Many parents often find that having children can surface wounds from their own childhoods. Memories from the past may re-emerge unexpectedly, sometimes inspiring fondness but other times bringing up pain. Not only do our children inadvertently bring us back to our own experiences growing up, but they can also serve to confront us with our own current edges of personal growth. I once told new expectant parents that having a child is often akin to carrying a constant mirror. That mirror shows both the depths of your infinite love, as well as the darkness of where your heart stops itself in closure. As with any mirror, we can choose to look or not look.

Since becoming a mother, I have stumbled upon unexpected and difficult pockets of remembrance and personal confrontation many times. Often my equanimity is tousled like a fierce wind blowing up leaves I didn't even know were there. Sometimes parenting stirs up new winds that I can tame, and other times I'm blown to the brink of utter exasperation. At these more difficult times, the shadow within the mirror image can become far from graceful, calm or centered.

When the Poop Literally Flies

How quickly the tides can change when negotiating with our children! There are moments when we are forced to wrestle with impatience and frustration, shallow breath or a raised voice. As a new mom, I often had the experience of not-knowing how to curb the fire of a tantrum. I was at times surprised by my own fiery response. With a bit of self-observation, I aspired to do the dance of mindfulness: working to slow down, reach out, make eye contact, and speak patiently and lovingly.

On a normal summer day at the grocery store I found myself up against my edges. A diaper needed to be changed, and a struggle towards the bathroom stall ensued complete with kicking toddler in my arms. The poop had exploded beyond the diaper, and one of my boys was trying to hit me in the face. He told me, he "wants to sit in his poop" and he "wants to leave poop all over his clothes" and how dare mama try to change his diaper. We barely made it to the bathroom stall in the midst of the screaming and full-blown tantrum. Before I knew it, we were on the floor with excrement smeared everywhere.

All of the sudden there was a snap in my patience and I had to force my son to be still so I could clean him. I'd lost any semblance of composure and I was yelling, just like my child. It felt like falling into a pit of mutual misery where we were both flailing to maintain control. In moments like this, I'm taken to a place where I simply want out. I wanted to fight the moment because I'd reached my limit of tolerance. I didn't want to deal. I'd had it. I was done. I was angry. Instead of holding the line of compassion and sanity, I'd headed off the deep end as I wrestled with excrement and my son.

Later, as I reflected on the incident, I realized I could have handled the situation differently if I had only paused to dig deep in order to find my inner resources. Sometimes this feels impossible in the moment. It is yet another skill that parenthood had invited me to hone.

So What to Do?

The incident in the grocery store offered me a painful window into a facet of parenthood too often reserved for the sidelines. We don't talk enough of the moments when we are faced with our own raw edges. I wanted to connect more about those moments when my ability to respond with equanimity was taxed to the brink. After losing it in the grocery store bathroom, I felt not only embarrassed, but also guilt-ridden. I'd let myself and my son down. How did other parents cope? What was the "right" response?

The moment in the stall with poop flying had required my holding a firm boundary. It was a moment pointing to a complexity of the most painful sort. It was of course unacceptable that I let my son drip excrement along the grocery aisles. Had his mess been confined within his diaper, perhaps there could have been the choice to wait until home. But it was the messiest of situations. Of course he needed a diaper change. The whole ordeal was utterly irrational. There are times when humor doesn't work and reasoning doesn't work. There are times when a kind voice is lost to the wind. So what to do?

We as parents are tasked with holding a firm and necessary boundary, while doing it with a strongly expressed loving force. There is a moment of artfulness if this can be mastered. It can also be a moment of mutual learning and connection—if only we as parents can hold the line of boundary steeped in loving presence. The question for me became: Could I be free of the need to "react" in my own offended or impatient ways? Could I move beyond the immediate triggers in order to dig deep and find my own reserves of patience and sense of humor? Could I handle frustrating situations with levity, along with compassion?

It wasn't just the moment in the stall that was prompting these questions. Daily, I was bumping up against challenging moments and scrambling to respond with integrity. I quickly saw that I could grow if I stayed with the mirror that my children offered me. I could respond differently next time. I could return to the moment and talk it over with my children. I too could say, "I'm sorry" and "I was sad and frustrated, just like you." In this way, I could demonstrate personal responsibility for my actions and admit when I too "wasn't being nice."

What the Mirror Reflects...

Because the infinite love for my child is also a constant mirror, so then too is the pain of not living as fully in the light of that love. Herein is one of the most marvelous conundrums. We can grow if we learn to sit with the raw pain of letting ourselves and our children down. We can connect with the vast heart impulse that our children beckon more alive in us, and practice growing ever more into that impulse. The mirror simply shows us where that impulse stops short of its potential infinity.

It's no wonder one of my most difficult moments with one of my sons was in a bathroom stall with poop flying everywhere. What a gift to deal with so much literal *shit!* Never again will so much literal excrement be in my face than during this period of mothering young ones. In that moment, I had a choice. I could face it, deal with it, and stay connected with my impulse to grow. Or I could shut down, turn my back and run past the rough spots. I could choose to gloss over the baggage that was dragged up to the surface. At these times, it often seemed easiest to assume none of this was about me. I could have thought, "This is all about my irrational two-year-old. Now, let's move on..."

Like putting money in a piggy bank, over and over again motherhood was tasking me with doing my own inner work and taking time to reflect. This time, I needed to take time to feel my own grief and sadness about my limitations. I needed to face the parts of myself that get 'fed up' to the point of cracking into my own tirade. I needed to accept the point where my inner dialogue and response gets stuck in "I'm so sick of this! Get me out of here!"

With a bit of reflection, I saw that I needed to attend to my own emotions. I could then re-enter the sacred ongoing bond with my children. That way, I knew I had done the work required in order to show up as present and as clear as possible in the next moment. Most importantly, I needed to bring the wrestling with my own shadows to light. In this way, I could bring more of my experience into the light of loving truth and acceptance. And—I could then reflect this back to my child.

The Invitation

Reflect on a recent time when you lost your patience.

How did you respond?

Identify what you would like to do differently, if anything, next time.

In what ways is your child a mirror for you?

Whatever arises, take time to reflect on your internal reactions and responses.

Not Knowing, Bearing Witness

"When we bear witness... the right action arises by itself. We don't have to worry about what to do... Once we listen with our entire body and mind, loving action arises."

~ Bernie Glassman, Zen Buddhist Teacher

The early years of parenting have ushered in a breadth of experiences and emotions unlike any other period of my life. Although many of the moments I've chosen to write about reflect challenge, there are always the daily doses of unbridled joy and fun. There are periods of calm mixed in with necessary periods of tumult and friction. The times my husband and I welcomed our children as newborns always brought with it the awe of bonding with a precious new life. Each child brought his own unique imprint into the world. Each time a new member joined the family, that joy was also coupled with the pain and heartbreak of watching our sons respond to a world turned upside down.

Attending to Multiple Needs

Each time I gave birth, the complexity of parenting deepened as I juggled multiple needs that simply could not be resolved in the same moment. Chris and I often huddled in the evenings, trying to reckon with what to do when each family member seemed to have competing needs. What could I do when the newborn needed milk or soothing at the very same moment that the older boys were struggling and needing attention?

We embarked on a process of soul-searching. Why was it that the nuclear family model didn't seem to work on many days? With a newborn in particular, we needed help and a lot of it. Perhaps most poignantly, we needed help in the moments when our sons were throwing tantrums and choosing new undesirable behaviors in response to changes in our family. I needed help when repeatedly woken up in the 4 or 5 o'clock hour by an anxious three-year-old undergoing sleep regression in response to the birth of his new brother. I needed help resolving the strange feelings of guilt I was dealing with for disrupting the previous family balance by daring to give birth again.

One of my sons asked me to please put his brother back in my belly so that "he didn't have to feel so alone." It was heartbreaking. I knew he was sad, and that it was difficult for him to witness me spending so much time tending to his baby brother. But his sadness was not only expressed in words. There were moments when the blankets were deliberately pulled off of the sleeping baby, or when the baby's legs were yanked on during a moment of breastfeeding. I remember one day I was trying to water the plants while carrying my newborn. All the while, my other little one was following me trying to make me drop his brother. When that plan failed, he began pulling leaves off the plants and scooping dirt out of the pots and onto the carpet. The message was clear. *This transition was hard!*

During these periods of intense life transition, my primary goal was to attend to each situation with compassion for the underlying emotions while also holding a line as to what was acceptable. How could I offer a longer leash than usual given feelings of sadness and confusion while also figuring out where to draw the appropriate line in the sand about when enough is enough?

The Bottom Line: Change Is Indeed Hard

It was during these moments of family transitions that I read psychologist Marshall Rosenberg's *Nonviolent Communication* pamphlet on raising children. I needed to craft a response strategy. How could I meet and greet the difficult emotions arising in my children and normalize them? How could I maintain some semblance of balance and boundaries while also keeping my newborn safe? If only I was attending to just the behavior and not all the underlying emotions! And if only the underlying emotions were simple and simply resolvable!

Each day unfolded another layer of an onion of complexity. Intense swings of love, silliness, and affection mixed with confusion and frustration. All the while, there were the normal ebbs and flows of adjusting to a new situation. There was the normal, lovely everyday reality: books were read, bikes were ridden, naps were taken and playdates maintained. I focused on bearing witness to the growing pains, and meeting all members of the family from a place of patience. I didn't always succeed. Change was indeed hard.

Enter the Zen Peacemaking Principles

As I navigated the emergent waters of jealousy and conflict amongst siblings, I recalled learning about the Zen Peacemaking Principles when I'd been a student at Naropa University. Bernie Glassman, a Zen Buddhist teacher and founder of the Zen Peacemakers, had led me to three central practices in being a peacemaker: *Not Knowing, Bearing Witness and Loving, Skillful Action.* According to the Zen Peacemaking Order, peacemaking requires these principles. When we are working to restore peace in our households, we too can remember that not knowing the answers is acceptable. As parents, we do not have to be all-knowing.

Keeping the Zen Peacemaking Principles in mind offered up new insights on working with difficulty as I responded to the daily bantering and outbursts. *Not knowing* helped me to tap into trusting the mysterious processes at work, even when these processes were painful. If I allowed myself the space to be confused, perhaps I could open up avenues for new and different responses to any given situation. Confusion and disorientation were certainly bringing me out of my comfort zone and into the unknown. Maybe this wasn't such a bad thing? After all, sometimes the comfort zone doesn't allow for growth.

It helped to come to my children daily with a sense of curiosity. I could listen more deeply if I didn't assume that I knew what was going on. Sometimes the best thing I could do was simply to slow down and witness my children, myself, my reactions and my children's reactions. It reminded me of *bearing witness,* which from a Buddhist perspective points to not turning away—even when the moment is difficult. It points to staying present as well as bringing your full presence to any situation. It points to listening deeply and bringing a sense of empathy and compassion to moments of challenge. *Bearing witness* invited me into a realm of deeper seeing where I could try to look beneath and beyond each difficult situation as it arose. If I slowed down to look deeper, I often found that angry behaviors were originating from a place of pain and hurt.

I was learning as I went—and it was hard. I often felt that I was failing, not able to give any of my children what they really needed. The third Zen Peacemaking Principle, *loving, skillful action,* didn't always manifest as clean and clear. How could I be firm yet also full of love simultaneously?

It was a recurring invitation. I still didn't know the precise answer—but I could remember that not knowing the answers was okay. Not knowing what to do was okay. Fumbling was also okay. I was learning. I could turn the experience of not knowing into a freshness of perspective. My curiosity could then fuel my responses. From there, I could witness what was unfolding with less judgment.

When in doubt, I committed myself to taking root and refuge right there in each moment of inhaling and exhaling. The breath was always available to remind me to simply witness the unfolding of a moment before I reacted. With a clearer head and more space in my lungs, I could then respond with fresh perspective—ready to greet whatever came.

The Invitation

Weave the Zen Peacemaking Principles (Not Knowing, Bearing Witness and Loving, Skillful Action) into your own family life, especially during moments of transition or conflict.

Be curious. Ask questions as if you truly don't know.

Bear witness not only to your children's actions but also to your own reactions.

Identify what loving, skillful action is for you when relating with your children.

Know that it likely changes with each situation.

Beginner's Mind

"Having a beginner's mind means having an attitude of openness, eagerness, and freedom from preconceptions when approaching anything...

It is that delicious state when you are sure of nothing, yet completely fearless, totally available to the moment."

~ Paramahamsa Nithyananda,
Indian Spiritual Teacher

I am one of those women who is always looking for new insight around being a parent. I have often asked myself, *What is needed now?* It was like doing a deep search into a toolbox, while not being sure what the right tools were. I'd looked to the Zen Peacemaking Principles for guidance. Now it was time to turn to the Buddhist notion of *Beginner's Mind.*

Perhaps "beginner's mind" was another insight I could weave in during difficult moments in my household? There was an unsettling cycle of sibling conflict, the resulting injury and sadness, and my subsequent frustration and exasperation. The cycle seemed to play itself out over and over again. I tried patience. I tried speaking kindly. It all seemed to no avail. The cycle continued.

As mothers, most of us encounter moments in family life where things are not running smoothly. I at times felt like no matter how many times I'd said something, the same unsettling patterns would still play themselves out. There was the struggle over sharing toys or food. There were days when everything felt like a power struggle, even the simple things like getting on shoes or brushing teeth. If you have more than one child, there are likely ongoing sibling conflicts—some superficial, some deep. If you have boys, you may like me be constantly mitigating physical energy and aiming to create safe spaces for the expression of this energy. Some of the difficult moments are rooted in routine developmental growing pains. Other times, the challenges may run deeper with more complex origins.

As my boys grew into toddlers and beyond, day in and day out I found myself constantly saying things like *No. Please don't. What are you doing?!* There was tripping, ear-pulling, the throwing of toys, and even "accidental" body slams while pretending to 'fight dragons.' The mantra *"connect, even when frustrated"* surfaced over and over again in my awareness. Connect. Even when frustrated. I'd resort to all sorts of shenanigans, including taking time-outs for myself to get away from the madness. Some days, nothing seemed to work to assuage the constant banter.

Help! We're Stuck in a Negative Cycle

While the constant banter was indeed part of my reality, there were certainly times when cooperation took root. Often, the ceaseless energy of my three boys would spin a dynamic web of wrestling, bed jumping or fort building. Their ideas for play together were unbridled. When things were smooth, I was often reminded of butterflies. They could flutter from one activity to the next, never stopping. They would manage to travel in all directions and on all planes.

There would be laughter and silliness mixed in with the constant motion.

However, there were times when my boys seemed to get stuck in a negative cycle. When they couldn't find a flow together, I worried that my parenting strategies and responses had become painfully stale and ineffective. We would get stuck. I would get stuck. Conflicts would repeat themselves and I'd repeat the same futile responses. So what to do? I couldn't handle one more squabble about sharing that truck or ball. I couldn't stand to hear myself say "please take a break and come back when you are ready..." one more time. And then it struck me one day—*Beginner's Mind!*

Like a dog barking from the bottom of a very distant well, I heard a crackle of inspiration. What if each day I chose an orientation of inquiry? I could practice letting go of any storylines that I'd created about my children's behavior. I could imagine I was walking into an entirely new situation each time I approached the same old conflict. Even though only five minutes may have passed since my last moment of intervention, what new response could I bring now? And now? And now?

As Indian spiritual teacher Paramahamsa Nithyananda says, having a beginner's mind means embodying an attitude of "eagerness and freedom from preconceptions when approaching anything." Beginner's mind points us towards the space where the mind doesn't know what to do, yet in this space there is a quality of fearlessness where we can be totally available to the moment.

Starting Fresh

Ultimately, I wanted to transform the cycles of unsettledness in my family life. I wanted tools for working with difficult moments and emotions. I wanted to somehow break negative patterns. Practicing beginner's mind invited me to set aside preconceptions when approaching anything. The space where the mind does not know what to do is actually something to celebrate. Maybe I could find a freedom here. Rather than scramble for an 'appropriate' or 'effective' response to whatever chaos was arising, I could instead take pause.

This way, I could start from a renewed place. I could practice seeing my children with new eyes, over and over again. I could throw strategy out the window and be spontaneous with my responses. Rather than feed into a recurring pattern, I could choose more availability to the present moment. We can act as if we've never experienced anything like it before. Because, truly, we haven't!

Tapping into beginner's mind felt like entering a wide open space where creativity could thrive. It was the antidote to habitual response. When I resorted to routine reactions, I often felt I was actively feeding the cycle I was trying to interrupt. Beginner's mind reminded me of the space that is always there to *choose differently.*

I was reminded of my boys' energy when they are at their best together, in a flow. In these moments of mutual playfulness, they are pure joy. Moving from one moment to the next, they are open, free and eager. With the image of my boys at play in mind, Nityananda's quote on beginner's mind struck me in a different way. *"It is that delicious state when you are sure of nothing, yet completely fearless, totally available to the moment."* Couldn't I too bring a playful openness to the present moment? This indeed was the cycle I wanted to feed.

The Invitation

Try a practice of "beginner's mind."

What would it look like if you embodied an attitude of openness, eagerness, and freedom from preconceptions when approaching anything?

Let go of any storylines you may have adopted about certain behaviors.

After a pause, practice bringing a spontaneous response to each situation.

Negativity Simply Becomes Food

"Then negativity simply becomes food, pure strength. You no longer relate to negativity as being good or bad, but you continually use the energy which comes out of it as a source of life so that you are never really defeated in a situation."

~ Chogyam Trungpa Rinpoche,
The Myth of Freedom

On one particularly hot summer morning, I told one of my sons that I was angry at him. I wish I could say that I'd said it in a calm, measured way. But no. Instead, I'd yelled. It was a low parenting moment. I promptly said, "Mama needs a break" and went into the bathroom and locked the door. It was a moment when I'd been pushed to the edge, and I felt my son had gone too far. I had really lost it, and I expected my husband Chris, who witnessed my outburst of anger, to agree that I had let our family down. He instead said, "At least our son sees that it is okay to feel angry. At least he sees what is real for you. He knows the very real effect of his actions. You didn't sugarcoat anything. You were authentic with your feelings. You showed him that moms also need space and a break."

The incident invited me to reflect on my own anger and frustration, and also forced me to confront my own discomfort with expressing what felt like "negativity." Chris however reminded me that perhaps a more useful way to look at any difficult situation within a family is whether we have acted authentically. This doesn't mean letting ourselves throw tantrums, just because we feel like it. But it does mean owning our anger, exhaustion and intense frustration when it arises. It means not turning away or glossing over the complex emotions that surface in any given day raising our children. It means modeling accountability by acknowledging what we could have done differently and apologizing if feelings were hurt. As author Brene Brown says, "I will not teach or love or show you anything perfectly, but I will let you see me, and I will always hold sacred the gift of seeing you."

Working with Negativity

Parenthood was ultimately teaching me about working with 'negativity.' It was also teaching me about my own expression of anger in response to so-called 'negative' behaviors. In my family we often talk about how "our love includes everything," even the frustration and mutual mistakes. It was a time of multiple transitions, with a new home and new schools affecting each of us and wires were frayed all around. I'd shared my experience with another mother and she reflected that she too had been working with how to best parent while under stress. "Motherhood is a humbling series of failures," she said. I concurred, while also acknowledging that the point of perceived failure is often a doorway to true transformation. The questions for me became: *What do you do when you're standing at this humbling doorway of failure and mistake? How do you dance with negativity?*

Chogyam Trungpa, a Tibetan Buddhist meditation master and lineage holder, had an answer for me. He'd written that it was possible to cut through conceptual ideas such as "good" and "bad" or "light" and "dark," instead entering a non-dualistic state. "Negativity" didn't have to be "bad." It was in this non-dualistic state where "negativity simply becomes food, pure strength." In his book, *Myth of Freedom*, he writes:

You must not make an impulsive move into any situation. Let the situation come, then look at it, chew it properly, digest it, sit on it. Frivolousness means reacting according to reflex. You throw something and when it bounces back you react. Spontaneity is when you throw something and watch it and work with the energy when it bounces back at you. Once you are emotionally worked up, then too much anxiety is put into your action. But when you are spontaneous, there is less anxiety and you just deal with situations as they are. You do not simply react, but you work with the quality and structure of the reaction. You feel the texture of the situation rather than just acting impulsively.

I considered what this might look like in my own life. For example, during our bedtime routine at the end of a somewhat long day, my son threw his toothbrush. He did it again. He then pushed his brother. He then threw the toothpaste along with the toothbrush. The dialogue between us went something like: "Are you trying to make me mad?" "Yes, mama." And then, I do get mad, toss the equanimity out the door, and resort to acting like a four-year old myself!

This was indeed reacting according to an agitated reflex. This was clearly *not* reacting with spontaneity.

This was most certainly impulsive, and I was definitely "emotionally worked up." As parents, what do we do when we are consistently pushed to the edge of what feels tolerable in terms of 'negative' behavior? How can we work with it? Where is the love when we fly off the handle? What do we do when it feels like a continual mess?

Intimacy with Everything

Eventually I remembered something Zen teacher Dogen Zenji said: "Enlightenment is intimacy with everything." It reminded me of what Trungpa had invited me to consider—that I didn't have to orient to things so definitively as "good" or "bad," "positive" or "negative." I could somehow integrate all of this: the letting myself and my family down, the experience of failing, the loss of control, the dualistic mind that self-judges, the wrestling with shadows, the impatient mother who doesn't want to deal with a four-year-old's antics.

What if I didn't have to fall into labeling anything (including my own actions) as "good" or "bad?" Rather, this whole process of working with 'negativity' could be used as food for my dance in life, energy for my continued unfolding and relationship with what is. I was reminded of certain Tibetan Buddhist paintings where the 'negativities'—the painted demons or a crown of skulls surrounding a head—served as ornaments along a spiritual practitioner's path. What if I too related with 'negativities' in this way? I could remember that all feelings are allowed, and all actions can be danced with. I could still set limits while also welcoming the full spectrum of emotions.

Most importantly, I could stay close and connected with my child when 'negative' behavior was booming. I could do this because I'd done the work of staying intimate with my own negativities. Not avoiding. Not ignoring. Not glossing over. Not pushing away. I can be angry, too! And still I can work to restore calm, not from a place of this being 'right' or 'wrong,' but from a place of spontaneous dance through whatever is being tossed at me in these crazy moments of parenting.

The Invitation

Consider how "negativity" arises in your household.

How might you "dance with negativity" and stay intimate with your own 'negativities?'

Rather than relating to negativity as 'good' or 'bad,'

consider how it can inspire you to grow.

The Borders of Choosing Love: What Place Does Anger Take?

"Conflict and tension are as much a part of the human condition as interdependence is.

There are times we have to have conflict, and tension has to exist to bring something else into being. But they have to coexist with a deep sense of connection and shared destiny."

~ Ai-jen Poo, American Activist
& Co-Director of Caring Across Generations

Over the years I've become a huge fan of Dr. Laura Markham, author of *Peaceful Parent, Happy Kids* and *Peaceful Parent, Happy Siblings*. I'm also a fan of her *Aha! Parenting* email updates, which are a constant gift arriving weekly in my inbox. She reminds me of my responsibility as a parent to regulate my own emotions, and to connect deeply with my kids. She signs off each of her columns with "choose love."

I too of course want to choose love. And of course my love is ever-present for my boys. It is always there as a container within which we live. Yet no matter how vast my love is, there were some days when acting from a place of love felt harder than others. I went through a time when I needed to reconcile the vast spectrum of emotions that were possible as a parent. Sometimes when my sons physically fought with one another, I would see red. I often found myself riding along that border of choosing love and I wanted to know what place anger takes. *How do we as mothers express the energy of anger from a place of union, connection and integration?*

Energy Needed to Set Boundaries

The Hindu goddess Kali came to mind. She is the fierce companion to Shiva, the consort to "being-bliss-consciousness." She points to the dynamic aspect of creation, even when she is also at home destroying what needs to be destroyed. She reflects a creative integration of seemingly conflicting energies. She is a protector yet she can also be fierce. If something needs destroying, or if a boundary needs to be set, she'll do it, and she'll likely also wield her sword while dancing.

I too was doing a daily dance with my sons. It's a dance of protection as well as a dance of aiming to cut through harmful actions. My anger was often rooted in the energy required to set boundaries. Sometimes, when I looked carefully, there was a deep sadness beneath it. There was also the texture of indignation: the interpretation of my children's actions as a personal affront. Why did they keep pushing boundaries? How could they keep hurting each other? How could one put his foot out to trip the other? Why did the other insist on twisting the baby's ears? There was confusion. How should I respond? What did each child need? How on earth could I keep 'choosing love,' even in the moments when one of my children is being harmed?

One thing I've landed upon is that choosing love doesn't mean rejecting anger and all the accompanying subterranean emotions. Choosing love does mean prioritizing compassion as often as possible while also holding a space for all emotions arising. Choosing love also means staying intimate. It means staying connected, even when setting a fierce boundary. Certain tensions do require a more dynamic response. The key is to be in a dance of integration of opposing energies. For example, we can dance with equanimity, even when working with the opposing energy of anger. We can dance with acceptance, while also working with the opposing need to shift something in order to set clear boundaries.

Finding Union Amidst Tension

When I paid attention with the above insights in mind, the dance with one of my sons revealed a different narrative. Through a constant testing of boundaries, I heard him asking for reassurance. His actions were asking, "Will you love me even when I'm anxious and confused?" "Will you join with me even in these sticky places?" "Will you stay with me even when I push you away?" "Do you still love me even when I make mistakes?" The answer must be yes—even when coupled necessarily with the energy of self-protection or protection of my other children. We can always begin with a peaceful and patient joining, rooted in our deep connection—while also being prepared to dance into the more tricky realm of fierceness. We can hold the proverbial sword that slices though ignorance: not to harm, but to stop the rise of nonsense and needless suffering.

The "low road" of parenthood shows up when we succumb to isolation and punishment. It is when the path of union has been lost. I remember a time when one of my sons said, "You don't love me!" In that moment, he pointed me to the places in my heart that had yet to relax into my infinite capacity to love. He shined light on the places within me not yet residing in ultimate union and intimacy with everything that was arising, particularly the messy, miserable, frustrating moments of parenting. He would mirror this place to me again and again until I met him from a place of no-separation, from a place of ultimate and unconditional acceptance, free of conditions.

And so I danced my way into expressing the energy of anger from a place of union and integration. The only "space" taken must still be together in spirit— where time slows and response can be masterful. The only pain results from how close we want to be but haven't yet grown into yet. As author and activist Ai-jen Poo says, "There are times we have to have conflict, and tension has to exist to bring something else into being. But they have to coexist with a deep sense of connection and shared destiny." Aha! Indeed.

The Invitation

Do you agree that there are times when conflict or tension are necessary in your family?

Reflect on when and why tension arises.

How do you or might you set boundaries while also staying connected and in close relationship?

What does choosing love look like during your days?

Prioritize compassion as often as possible while also holding a space for all emotions arising.

Where You Place Your Attention Becomes Your Experience

"Humans love drama. We revel in the excitement of risk and conflict, competition and difficulty. We love to talk about what's wrong. A time has arrived in human history where we must find that new trajectory that allows us to raise our children in ways that make happiness, confidence, inner peace, cooperation and greatness the exciting measure of our priorities."

~ Howard Glasser, *All Children Flourishing*

I adjusted to the natural ebbs and flows of familial rhythms. Some seasons were smooth and sweet like honey, where joy and cooperation were the norm. I could simply enjoy life with my constant companions. Other seasons, as I've written about here, ushered in the hard spaces. In the times of challenge I knew I needed time and space to step back from the daily dramas in order to reflect and find a sense of renewal. Hatha yoga gifted me with those opportunities, and in the quiet evening spaces of practice while the boys were sleeping, I would remember lessons shared over the years from many amazing teachers.

Missing the Good Stuff

One such lesson came from Sofia Diaz, an amazing Hatha yoga teacher. She is someone who helped me connect my yoga practice with the rest of my life. She would often say, "Where you place your attention becomes your experience." She would repeat this mantra during a class with 'challenging' yoga poses. It was the perfect advice for those moments when most of us were internally cantankerous about burning muscles, a feeling of fatigue, or the desire to rest and avoid a hard pose. *"Where you place your attention becomes your experience,"* she'd tell us. Her invitation was to notice all the beautiful things happening, even when we were uncomfortable, physically fatigued, or about to lose our balance.

Instead of focusing on the discomfort or self-doubt, I began to practice appreciating each moment, even when I was uncomfortable. It didn't mean that I ignored the difficulty, but instead I chose to place my attention on the dimensions of my experience rooted in enjoyment—rather than avoidance or frustration. Sofia often encouraged us to notice our toes or ears. Even when the rest of the body was working overtime, she would remind us to focus on those parts of our bodies (and experience) which were usually just fine. I began to wonder how this insight could translate into my parenting journey.

What if where you place your attention becomes your experience, even with your children? For a large part of my early years as a mother, I had too often been yanking my attention to all the troubles between my young boys: the grabbing of toys, the too rough wrestling matches, the crying and conflicts. The exhaustion of it all had rendered me too often strung out. I was working so hard to usher in an experience of peace and kindness, I was actually missing the many moments where peace and kindness were actively at play!

I knew that it was important for me to dive deep and work with what, at times, felt "negative." I'd learned lessons from that process that would last me a lifetime. There was a time and place for sitting in the fire and figuring out how to respond to conflict within myself and in my family. But there was also a time for looking around and being sure to take stock of all the wonderful things taking root. And, indeed, the good stuff was abundant. It was time to more deeply acknowledge it.

Focus on the Positive

Howard Glasser's book *All Children Flourishing* fell into my life at a perfect time. Glasser's insight on working with children is straightforward: *Focus on positivity.* It is about the "relentless pursuit and celebration of positivity." He suggests that by doing so, we as parents can purposefully nurture successes and greatness. That is, we can place our attention over and over again on what our children are doing kindly, generously, carefully, bravely, patiently, thoughtfully and responsibly.

Switching my perspective to place my attention over and over again on the smooth moments in the day - the kindness, the respect, the cooperation and generosity—began to transform my experience. Just like on the yoga mat, I could choose to focus on what can be identified as 'problems' or difficulty, or I can focus on what is naturally beautiful, life-giving, full of love, free of drama. These qualities of experience are ever-present; it is just that the gravitation to drama lures us, often on an unaware level. The magnetism to conflict can be powerful.

How on earth could I have missed something so obvious? Was I overly placing my attention on the "negative"? Was I worrying too much? I was not only deepening my own experience of distress, but also perhaps fostering more negativity. As I read Glasser's book, I realized that Sofia's teaching about where you place your attention becoming your experience also holds true in families.

Instead of over-focusing on the drama, I consciously switched the way I was paying attention. I softened my gaze in order to see the many quiet moments of sibling bonding, the gestures of kindness, the slow unfolding of cooperation and sharing, the collective giggle, the mischievous shared glances of solidarity while playing. And then I simply put energy *there*. I began noticing it outwardly, commenting more often on what I noticed and appreciated about how my children were kind, creative, thoughtful, helpful, and caring of one another. Instead of focusing on pulling out unwanted 'behavior weeds,' I was focusing more on watering the seeds of kindness and peaceful coexistence.

Instead of waiting to intervene when there was a conflict, I made sure to interject myself with positive reinforcement in the moments of smoothness. *"I noticed you shared that truck without even being asked!"* *"I see that you three have found a fun and creative game to play together!"* *"Wow! You cleaned up all by yourselves!"* *"You are really keeping each other safe and protecting each other!"* Once I started paying attention, the moments of smoothness were everywhere. My whole experience shifted. I felt happier—and I believe my children did too.

Remembering Basic Goodness

The switch in perspective has made all the difference in my experience of family life, while also engendering more inner wealth and confidence in all of us. Glasser's practice involves not getting drawn into giving our children greater responses or more animation for 'negative' behaviors. It is about not rewarding 'problems' with our energy, response or relationship.

As Thich Nhat Hanh says, "When mindfulness embraces those we love, they bloom like flowers." I realized my personal practices could play a role in fostering peace, both inner and outer. My own mindfulness practice or attention practice could shower positivity, positive reinforcement and loving words of encouragement on my children. It required a deep seeing, a looking beyond surface drama to the qualities of human greatness that reside in each heart.

The shift in attention did not make conflict go away. But it did soften my experience and helped me to see my children with more tender, patient eyes. It allowed me to live in a realm of more balance, where I could reside in greater appreciation for all the basic qualities of human virtue taking root. Just like in a challenging yoga asana, this moment in life too presented all sides. There was discomfort, there was frustration, and there was the need for balance and inner strength. There were physical and emotional limits confronted. There was connection. There was kindness. There were daily tender moments of my children learning how to be in the world, together.

I'm reminded of Tibetan Buddhist teacher Chogyam Trungpa Rinpoche's instructions on "basic goodness." Basic goodness is our human nature, he says. It is the underpinning of human virtue, always present. "We experience glimpses of goodness all the time, but we often fail to acknowledge them," Trungpa says. With a little intention, I could acknowledge the thousands of glimpses of goodness always underway. I could choose a practice of focusing on positivity—and I could choose to see the background of basic goodness as the ground from which all things can emerge.

The Invitation

Consider where you place your attention.

What is your experience of your children and your home life?

Make a practice of focusing on positivity and noticing 'basic goodness' at play.

Take time to look beyond surface drama to the qualities of human greatness that reside in each heart.

PART V

Love Is a Practice

"You don't need to justify your love, you don't need to explain your love, you just need to practice your love. Practice creates the master."

~ Miguel Ruiz, The Mastery of Love: A Practical
Guide to the Art of Relationship

Before becoming a mother, I had long reflected on what kind of person I wanted to be. Perhaps it was the conscientious example of my parents. Or perhaps it was my interest in spiritual practice and my desire to live intentionally. Whatever the origin, I knew that deepening in my capacity to love was an absolutely essential ingredient.

I entered into motherhood having no idea how much my heart would be stretched. Motherhood invited me to experience love as never before. Not only was my heart expanding, but I was also invited again and again to practice love when my patience was tested or my limits had been met. I was often tired, yet one of the lessons that emerged was that I could still practice love even when rest felt scant. I could make a practice of letting love shine through. At each step, my sweet boys were there, pulling on my heartstrings and showing me new ways to be in love.

Part V explores how love can be a slow and steady practice. My family was undergoing many transitions, and I was navigating questions of discipline. I was trying desperately to nourish the roots of kindness, even when other emotions seemed to be taking the reins.

Most importantly, I was growing a new muscle of staying connected and in deep relationship, even when things were difficult in unexpected ways.

Ultimately, as parents, we are living into the great endurance test of Love.

What carries us through the many hours, days, weeks and years of hard work? Love. What can sustain us when we're overwhelmed? Love. What can we return to over and over again—both in moments of joy as well as moments of uncertainty? Love. No more questions, no more looking. Just here: living, breathing, loving and caring. Just here: feeling the miracle of life while watching our children fall asleep.

Take a Bite Out of the Ego

"Much of motherhood, from the very first hour, carries the early warning signs of ego warfare.

I want to sleep. She wants to eat. I need to do this. She needs to do that. Not again. Again.

It can feel as though someone were eating you alive. And what is being eaten is your ego."

~ Karen Maezen Miller, *Momma Zen: Walking the Crooked Path of Motherhood*

My ego was being eaten by motherhood, and it was the most delicious bite of transformation yet. Devoured at 2 am. Downed with a drink of water at 5 am. Eaten again with breakfast at 9 am. Over and over again my needs and my children's needs bumped up against one another. Each time I thought I couldn't give anymore or do anymore, I'd find a new layer of possibility in myself. Somewhere since becoming a mother, I'd surrendered my attachments to what I thought I could never live without (attachment to sleep for one).

I often found myself awake in the middle of the night, tending to my children. Some midnight hours I'd find myself breastfeeding. Other hours I'd be changing a diaper or re-making a soiled bed. Other hours I'd be calming a nightmare. Whatever it was, I was slowly being worked on in mysterious ways.

In her book *Momma Zen: Walking the Crooked Path of Motherhood,* author and Zen Buddhist teacher Karen Maezen Miller writes about "ego warfare"—the process of working with attachments to how we want things to be. The constant needs of our children can feel relentless, and they can often pull us in opposite directions from where we think we want to be. I'd been experiencing my own crucible of "ego warfare," often pining for more sleep or personal time. But then one day after a few years of relative sleep deprivation, I recognized that a huge bite had been taken out of my ego while I was barely looking. Many spend lifetimes attempting to loosen attachments to the self and soften the ego, and here I was reaping a great gift of motherhood—the loosening of my own feisty ego. It did indeed feel at times like a part of myself was being eaten alive.

Letting Love Do its Devouring

My oldest son Rowan didn't sleep through the night until he was two years old. He had been five and a half pounds at birth, and I'd chosen to let him nurse at night when he woke up. One pediatrician had suggested he needed a little extra nourishment since he was so small. And so it was that this habit was formed, and it proved to be harder to kick than expected. His attachment to milk at night was a passion. I spent much of my first two years of being a mother running around ragged and sleep-deprived. I of course tried on many occasions to switch up our sleeping situation, to no avail. Finally, I surrendered. My child was not a deep sleeper. I actually wondered whether he liked sleeping at all. So it was.

I chose flexibility and adaptability as my response.

So what if I was up ten times at night? Somehow the experience of parenthood was eroding my habitual ways of identifying some things as good and others as "not good." Instead of attaching to the notion that "I need this and not that," I began to let go and just accept what was arising with less resistance.

I wondered if my ego was indeed being "eaten up," as Karen Maezen Miller writes about. I also wondered if that was such a bad thing. The Buddhist tradition relates the feeling of a separate "I" (sometimes called ego-consciousness) as being related to the strength of ignorance. A more conventional definition is that the ego refers to the self, especially as distinct from the world and other selves. The sleeplessness that had at first been the bane of my existence was now pointing me to unexpected insights. Maybe ditching some of my attachments and losing some sleep along the way wasn't such a bad thing after all.

I began to consider how I could surrender even one ounce of my self-absorption or self-preoccupation into service of another living being. Isn't that what we are doing as mothers much of the time already? I wanted to set myself aside in order to let the force of love do its work on transforming me. I wanted to let go of my attachments in order to better serve those around me. *Ultimately, I wanted to allow love itself to devour the parts of my existence that don't serve life.* And the path of motherhood was calling me over and over again to this surrender.

Practicing Love... Even When Tired

You see, love had been the experience I had tried to return to over and over again during those midnight wakings. It was the glue that kept me together. It was a stabilizing force when I felt I couldn't serve my child for even one more second. I decided to practice no resistance to the tiredness while also remaining open to glimmers of insight wanting to shine through. What if the tiredness actually helped to catalyze losing attachments to old habits that I didn't need anymore? What if the tiredness could whittle away at my perfectionism? What if it could usher in more humility? What if it could chip away at my ego in positive ways?

The tiredness of motherhood actually served to pull me beyond a certain holding pattern. This pattern at first revolved around the thought of "I'm tired and I'm just going to make all my bad habits worse because of it." Motherhood's exhaustion at first was like the straw that breaks the camel's back. It felt like I was being crumbled into a million pieces of oblivion where up and down, 2am or 6pm, didn't matter. The only thing that mattered—and that I kept being reminded of over and over again through how much I loved my kids—was Love. *Love* was the only force of reality that could truly sustain any semblance of sanity!

When the baby wanted milk every 45 minutes at 3 am, I often jumped out of bed screaming, "Feeding hours are over!" But then I would take a pause. I would feel my love for this child. Rather than drop into a heap on the floor, I could instead take a breath and tap into the love that anchors me. I could start over and try again. When I returned to the experience of love, it somehow dissolved my most irrational thoughts and behaviors. I could choose not to spin into self-absorption or even extended self-criticism or doubt. After all, there was no time for habits such as these! Sleep, and the baby, were calling...

Set Free by Setting Myself Aside

Over time it struck me what the discipline required to become freer in this lifetime is truly about. It is centered on the ability to make oneself more fully available to practicing an open communication with exactly what is, *even when it goes against what we think we most want and need.* The beauty is that when we do this as a practice, we make ourselves more available for love to work on us—and in turn to give away love as a constant. Perhaps my ego was indeed dissolving. Or perhaps sinews in my brain that serve to reinforce patterns of resistance were just loosening. It didn't matter. The point was to relax into the flow of letting go again and again into what is arising, without attachment to what I thought should be happening. Then, all of the sudden, something in my experience wasn't gripping so hard. I wasn't as attached to particular outcomes. Something was softer, more agreeable, more receptive and malleable. I had set myself free by setting myself aside in unabashed service of my child.

The force that fueled this potential was love. If I could surrender into just feeling the love for my children and let that be the guide—so much was possible! I could serve myself up in service to my children—and to life beyond myself and my individual ego. The experience of love reminded me of my interconnectedness and helped me to surrender even just an ounce of my selfishness. If I gave myself over to love, indeed love could do its mysterious work in my life. Most importantly, I could practice giving away love as a constant, even at 2am.

The Invitation

Consider your own relationship to being "tired."

How might the experience of being tired serve you?

*Has motherhood taken any "bites" out of your ego?
Consider the ways in which you have been
transformed for the better.*

*Let love devour the parts of you that don't serve life.
What does this mean for you, personally? What does
this look like in your life?*

Journal about this or make a list.

*Consider your own needs for self-care and how these
relate with your ability to live as your best self. What
self-care do you need in order to share the full extent
of your loving presence in your family and beyond?*

*What might it look like in your life to give away love as
a constant?*

Practice Bell Equals Baby Crying

"Love can change a person the way a parent can change a baby—awkwardly, and often with a great deal of mess."

~ Lemony Snicket, *A Series of Unfortunate Events*

One of the consistent times when I needed to "practice" love was in the middle of the night. It didn't come as naturally as it did during the day. In fact, it was quite the opposite. Those warm fuzzies that pervaded the daytime hours were quickly eclipsed as the night hours deepened. Patience, too, was easier to access when I was rested and sane—not at 3:53 am after a long day.

Since so many mamas always seemed to be tired (including myself!), I wanted to dig deeper into the experience of being "tired." I wanted to find a way to love it—and love my life in spite of it. For me, the exhaustion lasted so long I felt I had no choice but to try to look for the bright side. I kept looking for ways to soften the fatigue. Since I couldn't seem to break the cycle of sleeplessness, I looked for ways to shift my perspective.

There was one night when Braeden was still awake (and crying) at 3am, and I proceeded to self-medicate with chocolate, toast and tea. I was at my wit's end. "I need a break. I need a break. I need a break," I kept thinking to myself. And yet, there was no break in the traditional sense. My sweet baby was clearly awake and might be for a while. Maybe teething was the trouble. Or maybe it was colic. Maybe it was a stomach ache or maybe food allergies were at play. Who knew? And—hadn't I already learned all the lessons I needed to learn being up at night with my first baby? Why again? Why now?

A Midnight Lightbulb

"The wires in my brain aren't functioning properly," I remember telling Chris. I'd been so exhausted. At times I'd worried that I was "losing it." And yet somehow, being tired allowed for an opening of my perspective. Even though I'd been worried about the effects, the period of tiredness had helped me to distill one of the most important things in life: that love could shine through, no matter what.

It wasn't easy to arrive at that understanding. Sleeplessness was a recurring theme during those early years. Rest was scant and those nights awake often brought me closest to my limits. Daytime was one thing. I paired things down and kept life as simple as possible. It was easier to focus on practicing loving the simple joys of each day, letting love shine through a sleepy fog. But what about in the dead of night? How could I love even when I was at my limit of what felt possible? Could love shine through even when I was exhausted in the middle of the night?

One of my mantras had become "practice bell equals baby crying." The idea of such a "practice bell" was spawned by reading Buddhist meditation teacher Lama Surya Das's book *Letting Go of the Person You Used to Be*. In his book, Das suggests choosing a recurring sound throughout your days and designating it a "practice bell" in order to cultivate moments of greater mindfulness. This seemed like a perfectly valuable exercise during the daytime, but when 3am was tolling? That was a different story.

Being awake with a crying baby at 3 am generally ushered me into a bad mood, and the notion of "practice bells" seemed ridiculous. I just wanted to sleep. And yet Braeden's sweet confusion at my bad mood could still break my heart. I'd leave the room after helping him to sleep, realizing that his middle of the night cry was indeed a "practice bell" mirror for where I choose to shut down. His crying showed me that my reserves of compassionate loving had had enough and were morphing into an edgy restlessness.

But one night, a middle of the night lightbulb went on. I'd been reflecting on the "practice bell" that being awake in the middle of the night with a crying baby offered. I'd wanted to practice a loving response when the practice bell of baby crying sounded. But I couldn't seem to muster myself together. I'd just wanted a break. The inner lightbulb however helped me to see that the only break I actually needed was from the parts of myself that resisted staying with any given moment (for example, with my baby Braeden crying at 3 am). The "break" needed was actually from the parts of myself not yet integrated and fully accepted—like the part that wanted to toss myself out the window when I can't go to sleep. This part of myself was completely devoid of patience. It is the part of me that gets easily fed up, or the part of me that reaches a boundary and can't feel a way out.

Love! Even at 3am

The irony of this situation was that daily I worked to eke out small spaces for the non-mothering parts of myself (the writing, hiking, yoga parts, for example). *But all along the hidden quandary was that I needed more space for the parts that think they need a break and are at the edge!* In other words, I needed to spend more time with the moments of perceived "break-needing" in order to, through more intimate self-understanding and acceptance, move through these spaces to a deeper freedom and peace. This, my fellow mamas, is the fertile ground of change.

So 3am began to call me to a closer examination of just what it was I felt so "tired of." Really, when I sat still and spiraled deeper into this surface truth of "I am tired. I need a break," it was actually empty. At the core I was actually tired of nothing. It turned out to be all a story on the surface. Instead, the invitation was to remember to heed the call to stay seated in a heartbreaking love of this life—every precious moment. *I was only tired of the parts of myself that couldn't yet sustain this awareness of pervasive love recognition.* Without the delving this truth too would have continued to be obscured. Really, all of this was just profound light shed on parts of myself that weren't utterly dissolved in Love —even love in the midst of shrieking 3am baby.

Of course there are moments when breaks are in tall order. And of course sleep is essential for sanity and well-being. But the invitation here was about how to bring a practice of love into those moments when it had been a challenge to feel it. Persian poet and Sufi mystic Jalaluddin Rumi had once said, "Your task is not to seek for love, but merely to seek and find all the barriers within yourself that you have built against it." In the dark and quiet moments spent soothing Braeden at 3am, this rang truer than ever.

The Invitation

As Buddhist meditation teacher Lama Surya Das suggests, identify a sound that can be your "practice bell."

Decide what it is you want to practice.

Is it feeling your love? Deepening your patience? Expanding your capacity to slow down or listen?

Consider your own capacity to rest in "pervasive love recognition."

What factors in your life contribute to your experience of feeling love or the experience of being loved?

Nourishing the Roots of Love

"The supreme purpose and goal of human life is to cultivate love."

~ Ramakrishna,
Indian Mystic and Yogi

During the first three months of my middle son Braeden's life, a "toss up" quality prevailed. I felt like I was flailing at times under a hot sun that was broiling my new mama brain to smithereens. The summer heat coupled with my new family dynamics often gave way for disorientation and chaos to bloom, even with love simultaneously taking root. The frenzied moments of adjustment were like hot flashes in a pan.

There were hard moments of truth to move through. Tears shed. Voices raised. My oldest son wanted to send his little brother back to the belly. He would often say, *"Mama, could you please try to put him back in your belly so I don't have to feel so alone?"* It was heart-wrenching. Nonetheless, we stayed with difficult emotions and did our best not to force them into underground shadows.

The months went by, and I realized my dream of instant family bonding may not have been realistic. It was not destined to be "love at first sight" between brothers, and that was okay. But the seeds of love were there, of course. Slowly the baby's smiles and coos swayed us all into new places. Then suddenly we turned a corner into a new realm of emergent fondness between brothers, and an accompanying deep sigh of relief amongst parents.

Love: A Slow and Steady Practice

Love is a slow and steady practice, particularly in the early days of family bonding and adjusting. When a new baby arrives, all sorts of emotions and reactions can surface. As parents, we can help foster a practice of love amongst siblings, even when love doesn't always look as we anticipated. People (especially siblings!) don't typically fall in love overnight. Instead, an experience of love takes time, weaving through peaks and valleys and often complex terrain.

I'd come from a nuclear family where love had been my dominant felt experience. My brother and I adored each other and rarely had conflict. Even today, five minutes down the road, he's still one of my closest relationships. And I was one of the lucky children of the world who always felt loved by my parents. So the struggles in my own new nuclear family took me off guard. It prompted many questions.

As I watched my son work with the large transition of welcoming a new member of the family, I got to wondering about whether we can love what we want to initially push away? What does it take to go down that road? It's a tall order for anyone in life— especially a three-year-old. Can we practice seeing a reflection of someone like ourselves in those we don't like at first? "Look! He's a person just like you," I'd say to Rowan as we sat together with our new baby. When the baby cried, we'd talk about how he had feelings too, even if he couldn't talk about them.

Staying in connection, empathy began to surface. Love began to show a face that was more compassionate and less edgy.

The early days of welcoming a new brother showed me new dimensions of love. I saw that love could move its way through shadows to emerge in a place of acceptance. It just took time and it worked at its own pace. My oldest son and I did the dance of love and surrender and love and resistance in different ways, together. I was resisting the myriad expressions of his challenges, and he was resisting the presence of his new brother and all the implications therein. Family had indeed become a hard crucible of transformation—and I understood why so many have a hard time staying present through it all! And yet, love itself kept inviting me to settle in together, to be open to each new moment. Could I practice love even when I was discouraged? Could I trust the love in the family, even when it felt messy? The key was to keep coming back to my experience of love—and to understand that love looked a million ways. I just needed to keep returning to it as my ground.

And then, slowly, we entered into a new realm of practiced love between family members. We'd settled in! The toss-up and tumult had softened. Love had caught us in a moment of recognition. There I caught glimpses of my oldest smiling at his little brother in the rearview mirror. Like a slow blooming plant, the cultivation of love was underway. The key was to keep nourishing the roots of kindness and compassion, even when other emotions were momentarily taking the reins. I could stay connected, practice love—watering the roots of slow growth into a familiar comfort of being.

The Invitation

Nourish the roots of kindness and compassion, even when other emotions may be taking the reins.

Stay connected, even when things are difficult.

What was your experience of love growing up? What is your experience of love now?

Consider ways to 'practice' loving-kindness in your home.

Begin with small, daily gestures.

What about Discipline? Let Love Be the Guide

"You can't teach anyone anything without love, and without being happy with them."

~ Adi Da Samraj,
Spiritual Teacher, Writer and Artist

I spent the first few years of my childhood in Oklahoma City, Oklahoma, where my dad was a Lutheran pastor serving his first congregation. My early memories of my home life there are infused with just the sort of love I want to offer my own children. There were quiet moments on the back porch with our puppy, Kristi. There were many a moment spent on the play structure that my dad assembled for my brother Rob and me. My parents always seemed to be there to pick me up after a fall or to sit on my bed and listen to me when I needed the support. I was blessed with a happy childhood, and I daily feel the benefits of the presence that my parents offered to me. During our college years, I remember my brother and I sharing the recognition that we had actually been treated like gems by our parents. It was a gift that we continually express our gratitude for.

Alternately, my early memories of preschool in Oklahoma City are not infused with this same loving-kindness. The teachers would often pull out wooden paddles. They'd threatened to hit us with them if we didn't follow the rules or if we didn't lie down quietly on the carpet for "nap time." I remember lying on the carpet surrounded by all the other preschoolers, each of us motionless and often pretending to sleep, not moving for fear of retribution. If there was a rustling among the children, the teacher would take the wooden paddle and begin to smack her hand with it. It of course did the trick to get us all "in line." But was it the sort of discipline that was effective? What impact had it had on all of us? Had it served us for the better?

It was one of those memories that went underground until my own children were heading to preschool. I didn't want my own children to experience the threat of discipline by force as I had at school. I wanted to model much of what my own parents had practiced. I wanted to stay connected with my children, even when enforcing rules and boundaries. I didn't want to resort to fear and punishment. Ultimately, I wanted love to be the guide.

Luckily, I was able to send all of my boys to Alaya Preschool in Boulder, Colorado. Like Naropa University, it had been founded by Tibetan Buddhist meditation master and lineage holder Chogyam Trungpa Rinpoche. It was a magical place grounded in contemplative education principles, with compassion and acceptance serving as primary guiding principles. Through the contemplative tradition of observation, reflection and action, the teachers were always there to support the children in ways which were gentle, with just the right balance of firmness and structure. The focus was on social-emotional learning and learning to be together, in community. I always appreciated the cultivation of connection and empathy amongst the children. It was a school that wasn't afraid to speak about love in education. And when it came to "discipline," it was the opposite end of the spectrum from where I had lived out my own preschool years.

What about Discipline?

As my children got older and entered the preschool years and beyond, the challenges of parenting had morphed beyond coping with sleep deprivation or figuring out how to navigate the 24-hour needs cycle. Now I was thrown into a world with such questions as "What do I do when one of my toddlers is hitting another toddler?" or "What do I do when the kids are deliberately spilling their milk and then tossing their food on the floor?" What about how to deal with conflicts on the playground? And what about when rules were broken?

These were ultimately questions of *discipline*. I'd officially entered a new realm. There was conflict to deal with and there were broken rules to address. During the checkups with the doctor, the 'time-out' method was the front-runner of suggested techniques. Others recommended books such as Foster Cline's *Parenting with Love and Logic*. I did what many parents do. I observed others, tried on all sorts of approaches and learned as I went.

The word *discipline* is often associated with the uncomfortable space of trying to set boundaries and enforce limits. I knew it was the next huge bite I had to chew on. My sons were settling into their own personalities, ever freer and freer to choose their own responses and preferences. As they got older, my guiding questions centered around how to parent in ways that create the conditions for equanimity, balance and service to others and one's environment.

How could I transmit and translate all my personal philosophies into tangible parenting strategies? How could I foster sensitivity rather than hyperactivity? And even more so, how could I invite my children into a realm of mystery, reverence and self-transcendence? How did daily needs for discipline fit in?

The word discipline comes from the Latin *disciplina*, meaning "instruction given, teaching, learning, knowledge." Engaging discipline in this way, it was possible to feel into the prospect of daily disciplines pointing towards greater teachings I wanted to impart. Beyond the 'hardline' and the 'boundary,' perhaps there were realms of discipline that drew from the great wisdom traditions—calling forth our most realized understandings of relationship and love.

The Alaya Preschool Example

The boys' preschool was there to model the way early on. Rooted in the tradition of Shambhala Buddhism, the teachers acted based on the premise that there is a basic wisdom inherent in human experience, where bravery and fearlessness can be cultivated. Rowan's first year classroom at age two was called the Tiger classroom, the tiger referencing one of four "dignities" that Trungpa Rinpoche used as metaphors for stages on the path toward realizing our inherent goodness. Each "dignity" points to certain characteristics a practitioner develops in order to bring wisdom and compassion into daily life. At Alaya Preschool, it is never considered too early to begin instilling the human qualities of discernment, discipline, compassion and wisdom—toward which the four dignities point.

The Tiger points to contentment and discernment. Sakyong Mipham Rinpoche, Trungpa's son and the current head of the Shambhala Buddhist lineage, says, "As we slow down and consider our thoughts, words and actions with the question—*Will this bring happiness or pain?*—we become like tigers who carefully observe the landscape before pouncing. In looking at what to cultivate and what to discard, we are remembering our precious human life and deciding to use it well."

With my little ones, I had so often spoken of not hurting others' feelings, being gentle, and learning to be mindful of our bodies in space. Perhaps in line with the focus of the little Tiger class, I too could reflect with my children on what causes happiness or pain (both for ourselves and others). It was a practice of slow and steady cultivation of discernment and mindfulness of speech and action. Just like the contemplative tradition encourages, I could nurture reflection, slowing down, and time for consideration. Beyond just "impulse control" was also the potential of cultivating a foundation of compassion, reflectiveness and empathy.

Discipline: An Act of Love?

I'd been actively experimenting with what kind of discipline I wanted to infuse into my family rhythms when a friend invited me to join a 'conscious parenting' group which met weekly for six weeks. It was a perfect complement to what I'd been learning through my experiences with my children's preschool. I'd been trying so hard to create order in my home life. I'd been asking the big questions around the aim of discipline and education—and what kind of human experience I wanted to support and encourage. We discussed spiritual teacher Adi Da Samraj's book, *Discipline Is an Act of Love,* which pointed me towards the needed ground of discipline and structure. He saw them as a means of manifesting the seeds of right relationship between a child and family and then community.

Discipline Is an Act of Love reminded me that the art of true discipline lies in the ability to move a child into the "right adaptation to the law of life—which is to be in *relationship* to all beings and experiences that arise rather than in *reaction* to them." For Adi Da, the great insight to communicate to children was for them to "embody a heart converted to love." The trick was to help children return to a loving and happy state of being through releasing negative feelings. Part of attaining this was to help children connect with a sense of divine mystery. His book also reminded me that I needed to pay attention to my own reactions to whatever was arising. How was I responding? What space was I in? Was I myself living up to the invitation to "embody a heart converted to love?" It was a most welcome perspective on discipline. I'd been trying all sorts of systems and practices but had needed the reminder that the most important thing was to stay in connection, and stay rooted in love.

The basic task of true discipline then was to help children return to the understanding that "*they are loved and that they are also obliged to be Love,*" Adi Da wrote. If I lived my days of parenting with this discipline lens in mind and heart, could I create the condition for my children to feel their relationship with myself and others—and then beyond the family unit towards community and the natural world? What if the primary thing my children were reacting to through so-called negative behavior was their desire for connection? What if I was tending to the action and not the feelings behind the action? Each time I needed to redirect one of my boys, I tried to step back, consider causes, and check in with my own personal reactions before responding. I made a point of considering how connected or disconnected my children may have been feeling. What did they need? How could I make sure they knew they were loved, even when mistakes were made?

I focused on creating the conditions for balance through deepened connection. I made sure to tell my children I loved them every day. I remembered that every gesture in a day was an opportunity to maintain or deepen our connection. And every blip in the flow was a chance for me to assess whether the connection had been interrupted.

Was I Coming from a Place of Love?

"You can't teach anything without love, and without being happy with them," said Adi Da. It was just the advice I needed. Was I nurturing the deep threads of relationship? Was I taking a deep breath before flying off the coop after the toast was thrown for the fifth time in a week? In all situations, was I letting love be the guide?

Until I embodied equanimity, how could I expect my children to also live with a sense of equanimity? Children respond to our disposition perhaps more than our words. If I wanted to teach anything, perhaps I must first be feeling my love for my children, even in the very moment of pinnacle frustration. I could choose to take time to feel into my own experience—and ask myself if there was anything I was doing that wasn't serving my child when he was out of balance.

This perspective was a welcome infusion of new insight. Rather than creating a separation between myself and my children in the moments of intense frustration—when the most meaningful teachings were demanded of me—I could instead respond by staying in connection and remembering my love. Even if a "time out" was required, I could stay connected. And if that connection was severed, I was diligent about reconnecting as soon as possible.

Ultimately, I committed to letting love be the guide. Love indeed was a constant, but I didn't want to take it for granted. It was always there, but it also required some practice. Having children had expanded my heart a million times. I was asking again and again what love looked like and felt like in difficult moments. What was love like when my boundaries were being tested? What was love like when my children were breaking rules? How could love be the guide for all of my actions relating to discipline?

Sakyong Mipham Rinpoche says, "Using discipline to generate compassion, we leap beyond the fickleness of mood into the confidence of delight in helping others." Love was the force that made this leap possible. Discipline was the daily opportunity to generate compassion and inspire service and reflection. Now was the time to consider how to translate this understanding into daily responses. Now was the time to encourage my children too to "be love." With love as the guide, we whirled onward.

The Invitation

What is your relationship to "discipline?" How do you practice "discipline" in your family?

Consider ways to let your children know that "they are loved and that they are also obliged to be love."

Remember, every gesture of the day is an opportunity to maintain or deepen connection.

Identify three ways that you practice love already in your life, and three ways you would like to practice love more often.

Commit yourself to letting love be the guide - moment to moment, day to day.

Commitment: Saying Yes to the Crucible of Family Life

"And if you are looking for a crucible in which to heat compassion, marriage is a good one."

~ Susan Piver,
Author and Meditation Teacher

One day my mother handed me a piece of card stock paper with a poem typed on it. It looked vaguely familiar but I couldn't place where I knew it from. She said, "Don't you remember? It's from your wedding invitation!" I couldn't believe it. It had only been a few years, yet I'd completely forgotten about Susan Piver's poem "I Do?" It had been central to the spirit of how Chris and I had entered into our marriage vows all those years ago in Portland, Oregon. It was just what I needed to read again, except this time instead of the word *marriage* in the last line, I inserted *family life*. Indeed, if you are looking for a crucible in which to heat compassion, family life is a good one!

Family life did indeed feel like a crucible in which to heat compassion. In her poem *"I Do?"* Susan Piver writes that "In commitment we say yes to the unfolding, impenetrable arc of uncertainty. Love does not arise, abide or dissolve in connection with any particular feeling. Love has instead become a container within which we live." The poem goes on to describe how through a process of riding the waves of so many emotions, we "begin to live within love itself." Each time we extend beyond our comfort zones, the container of love is reinforced.

Family life and marriage had certainly become a place where I rode all kinds of emotions. Yet over the years, I'd simultaneously also relaxed into a container of love. The commitment to staying present and to keep showing up in the spirit of connection was the glue that often held it all together—especially in the difficult moments. As philosopher Friedrich Nietzsche said, "In family life, love is the oil that eases friction, the cement that binds us closer together, and the music that brings harmony." Yes!

The Fruits of Commitment

The word "commit" has its origins in the Latin *committere,* "to unite, connect, combine; to bring together." The commitment to one another, and to the broader values of love, intimacy and connection, is one of the forces that keeps Chris and I together. The gesture of commitment brings us back together as we weave our way through the ups and downs of our days. We often joke that since having children, the bridge to one another has gotten longer. Yet in spite of this, we're committed to doing what it takes to stay connected, even when we're both at opposite ends, trying to hold so many pieces together.

The commitment also translates to my connection with my sons. Over the years, through trial and error, we knitted the conditions for mutual trust. There were many messy moments where I doubted my path. On the parenting journey, it took time before I could see and feel the container of love and commitment at work.

One day, the role of commitment shone clear. There had been a clash between siblings, teetering on the edge of possible physical harm. I'd raised my voice and was feeling regretful. During a moment of space before re-joining the flow of family life, I took a pause. I knew apologies were in order on all sides. What helped to pull me back together in order to step forward as my best self was the experience of feeling married to the container of what had become a 24-hour-a-day family life crucible. I was wedded to the intentions I (and we) had set over the years per how we wanted to live together as a family unit. Here was where I could model humility—and I could own up to my own mistakes while also calling forth the best in my children.

We came together after the dust had settled to go over what had gone wrong. One of my sons asked, "Do you need a hug or anything?" He knew I had been upset. It had taken time, practice and patience, but slowly over the course of the years since each of my sons had entered my life we'd figured out how to communicate. The path to getting here certainly followed an "arc of uncertainty." It had required trust and a great deal of commitment.

One thing that helped our family clarify our commitments was to draw up a list of our family values. We used crayons and pictures, and together we wrote out the rules we agreed to live by. We posted the list on blue paper near our dining-room table so that we could see it every day. "Checking in" was on the list. It was a reminder that we all agreed to check in with one another after things had been difficult—whether there were hurt feelings or harsh words. Often this involved an apology. Other times it involved asking if other family members "needed anything." We also agreed that a check-in didn't have to happen immediately. It was reserved for when everyone was ready.

As Braeden and Kienan settled into preschool and Rowan settled into the grade school years, I noticed that there was finally a safety net that we seemed to relax into during and after our moments of conflict. It had taken years of trial and error, and staying with the difficulty and uncertainty. I'd practiced telling them again and again, "I love you no matter what... we all make mistakes." And I was sure to own my part of wrong-doing in moments of discord. We could now seamlessly express our anger, have our outbursts, and then share our disappointments and frustrations with what went wrong and what we wish went differently. Some days that process took longer than others and involved more fanfare. Other days, we were able to more quickly "push the green light button" to start over.

Along the way I'd learned that love itself had indeed become the container within which we lived. Through time, riding the waves of so many emotions, we had begun to live within love itself. Each time we were open with one another or stepped beyond our comfort zones, the structure of our familial commitment was indeed reinforced.

Saying Yes

Through commitment, we'd been given the greatest gift. When the commitment itself was fed and nourished, the container of love was there to support us. In family life, there were the crazy waves of joy and tenderness coupled with everything else. There was utter chaos. There was seemingly constant movement. There was noise. There were quiet moments of snuggles before sleep. There were fierce kicks to the shins right on the heels of the most precious moments of sibling love. And it all happened in any single day!

Family life at its closest is not for the faint of heart. There is no seclusion here, no retreating to quiet, familiar places. There are always fresh invitations, fresh wounds, and fresh moments offering fodder for appreciation and seeing with new eyes. There is always a wave to ride. Sometimes jumping off has its allure—but then I realize that the true gifts of staying committed only come to fruition over time and after the hard work of staying present, particularly through difficult spaces. The true gifts are only often revealed when we say a loud *Yes!* to the crucible of family life—hurt feelings, wild joy, messy chaos, deep love, arc of profound uncertainty, and all.

The Invitation

How is family life a crucible of transformation for you?

What are you committed to with your family?

Take time to revisit or set intentions, alone and together.

Practice noticing how love can be the container within which you live, even when working with uncertainty.

PART VI

Taking Pause: Making Time to Live into the Good Stuff

"We can purposefully pause during regular activities… We can choose to pause on the top of a mountain or in a subway, while we are with others or meditating alone.

The pauses in our life make our experience full and meaningful."

~Tara Brach, *Radical Acceptance, Embracing your Life with the Heart of a Buddha*

Perhaps one of the most poignant invitations of early motherhood has been to enter into a new realm of quiet poetry that is a day with the children. My little ones have a way of inviting me to look more closely at things I might otherwise gloss over. I found that if I took time to join my children in their playful wanderings, I too felt more joyful, spontaneous, creative and full of wonder.

I began to pay attention to the gifts of ordinary moments. I focused on weaving in more space for silence and mystery. It was time to count blessings, cut through the noise, and focus on what was important. I was discerning my own sense of purpose and responsibility as a mother.

For me, cultivating service, connection and empathy were top of the list. In a culture often moving too fast, I aimed to remember that we do have agency in how we live our lives and raise our children.

So I kept asking how could I integrate more time outside? How could I weave in more moments of getting lost in the small details of nature? How could I manifest more quality time with friends and family and less running around on the fly with granola bars gobbled in the back seat?

I wanted to swim like a turtle—carrying my experience of family and home as if there was always the possibility of finding stillness, silence and moments of awe. Through it all, I often heard the voices of my grandmothers. They beckoned me to reflect on what is important in the context of a full lifetime and beyond. What can we as mothers leave for the future? What do we want to focus on so we can live more fully into "the good stuff"? For me, it began with finding joy in the daily rhythms—and remembering to marvel at the little things, taking time to savor and play.

Divine Play & Savoring Life's Sweetness

"The Divine Mother is always playful and sportive. The universe is Her play. She is full of bliss."

~ Ramakrishna, Indian Mystic and Yogi

Perhaps the most poignant invitation of motherhood has been to enter into a new realm of quiet poetry that is a day with the children. I could enter the realm of the sacred when I attuned to the gentleness, inquisitiveness, curiosity and ecstatic joy in "common" daily encounters. All the while I knew that the choice was mine. I could enter into the sacred by seeing with fresh eyes, or miss the daily gifts being offered.

Seeing the Sublime - Even in the Parking Lot

I remember the day when my sons helped to open my eyes to how even the parking lot can be sublime. They had wanted to romp amongst parked cars and I, understandably, was resistant. Not only was I worried about safety, I also couldn't see the joy in walking the perimeter of a parking lot. As I beheld a vista of Hondas and Subarus, I was overwhelmed by tires and asphalt. I found myself wondering why I labeled time around a parking lot "not interesting."

Meanwhile my sons were living in the world as if it was the proverbial oyster, with almost everything inciting glee and wonder. Why did I shun car wheels, or not pay keen attention to such things as dirty snow, remnants of garbage on the ground, or ripped up paper in recycling bins? My littles ones helped me to look more closely at everything I might otherwise gloss over with relative disinterest.

My eyes had been conditioned to call some things "beautiful" and other things "ordinary."One spring day after a doctor's appointment, the parking lot became the vehicle for seeing the moon, sky and trees in the same light as that parked SUV with a crack in the window and a rusted tailpipe. Why differentiate? How did the parking lot become sub-par and cast off as a place to tune out, ignore? My boys had a knack for bringing their fresh, alive perspective just about anywhere. They could see the infinite possibilities for pleasure in unlikely places. They reminded me that the sublime is everywhere to be found, even in a parking lot. They reminded me of each moment's infinite expanse of possibility.

Beauty Is Everywhere

Indian philosopher Rabindranath Tagore says, "Beauty is omnipresent, therefore everything is capable of bringing us joy." Opportunities to be enchanted abound. It's like a practice switch we can turn on and off. I can *choose* enchantment, *choose* to rest myself in the beauty and sweetness of simply being alive. When doing so, I could then live my days like the unique poems they already are.

Each daily poem may have its ups and downs, ebbs and flows. But ultimately, when I parent, my young children remind me again and again that even the ant on the sidewalk or the browning leaf of a tree is worthy of wonder and awe. *Their curiosity and playfulness invite me to savor experience in a way that is beyond reason.* What better teacher of this than my children?

The way my children often tugged at me towards play also shed light on my conditioning. The moment in the parking lot showed me how I was labeling some things beautiful and others mundane. They also showed me my default towards experiencing life in linear ways. Rather than twirl in circles and bask in the little things, I was too often concerned with getting from point A to point B. And yet, playfulness and curiosity defies this conditioning. I walk straight lines and think "here to there," "this then that..." Children gallop in circles and serpentines, losing themselves to a moment when something interesting arises: bubbles in the waterfall, water splashing around rocks, a fly crawling up the window pane.

Playfulness Is the Path

American psychologist and "father" of play therapy, Charles E. Schaefer says that "we are never more fully alive, more completely ourselves, or more deeply engrossed in anything, than when we are at play." Why wasn't I following the invitation to play more often? Didn't a sense of playfulness with my children lead me to more delight and wonder? I was reminded of the Sanskrit word *lila,* which loosely translates as divine play or spontaneity. In Sri Aurobindo's

Philosophy of Social Development, lila's purpose is described as sheer delight. "This is the meaning of delight: Lila, the play, the child's joy, the poet's joy," he writes.

Almost daily my sons reminded me to savor and play. They could be enamored with just about anything. They pointed towards an effortless and playful relationship with life. They *are* life living itself joyfully. Some say *lila* springs from an abundance of divine bliss, rooted in creative energy. Here was the realm of no-agenda, spontaneous co-arising, surrendered presence into what just is. It was joyful, without effort, fun.

Often we adults want to 'move on' or 'move forward'—and play or curiosity becomes a diversion along the way. Yet over time I noticed that if I took time to join my children in their playful wanderings, it revealed my own abilities to be joyful, spontaneous, and full of wonder. Many young children model an absorption in the present moment that spiritual practitioners move towards through years of practice. And it is so simple: *Look at the bubbles! Look how they dance on my hands! Look how this water slips between my fingers! Feel the cool drops on your toes!* Why not toss your head back in utter delight and laugh along? The agenda can wait. And then, we can spiral back to ourselves, to our own infinitely playful, divine natures. All we have to do is bask here. Play. Spiral. Twirl. Be curious. Explore. Marvel at the little things. Smile at water falling as if it is truly a miracle, because, well, it is.

The Invitation

Reflect on how you differentiate between the 'mundane' and the 'beautiful.'

The next time you are in a parking lot, practice seeing with fresh eyes.

Take time to notice your child's curiosity and playfulness.

Pause the next time you find yourself focused on your 'linear' agenda of getting something accomplished or traveling from 'here to there.'

How might you instead join your child's play in the spirit of spontaneity, creativity and wonder?

Planting the Seeds of Awe

"The most beautiful thing we can experience is the mysterious."

~ Albert Einstein

Just as our children invite us to see and experience in new ways, so too do we profoundly contribute to their emerging worldviews and experiences of the world. As a student of philosophy in college, I remember Thomas Aquinas having said that "poets and philosophers are alike in being big with wonder." Philosophy, he said, arises from an experience of awe —a "feeling of reverential respect, an emotion inspired by the sacred or sublime." How could I encourage a sense of wonder in my family? Was I cultivating space for the mysterious? The sublime?

My Own Mother's Example

I credit my own mother with inspiring an experience of awe and wonder in my brother and me. Every family vacation oriented around an awe-inspiring place or event, and she modeled the way to experience wonder through her passion for learning and her zest for adventure. There was the August vacation one year planned entirely around the annual Perseid meteor shower. For this trip, Mom went to great pains to have us stay near a lake without city lights. That way, our family could sit together for a late-night meteor shower, viewing

203

shooting stars reflected in the water. Then there was the iconic "Trip West" with camping at the foot of the Grand Tetons. There was Yosemite. Yellowstone. The Badlands. There was even a month spent in Egypt when I was eight years old. While there, I slowly glided down the Nile River, making stops to visit temples and climb in the dark tunnels inside the pyramids. Mom was at my side, assisting me with taking my own photos and drawing my own artistic renditions of the sites we were seeing.

In her 70s, she still engages her passions for ancient history, archaeology, astronomy and photography. She star-gazes in dark fields late at night or drives down dusty dirt roads in Wyoming or Utah so she can snap the most iconic shot of the mountains. Mom is a woman who finds wonder in many things, and she was always there to share that experience with her children.

Ultimately, my mother gave me one of the greatest gifts. She showed me from an early age how to be captivated. She modeled how to relate to life beyond myself: to celebrate the past, the heavens, the stars and planets. With her mentorship, I could begin to feel my place in an order of things that was beyond self, time and space. I knew life was bigger than the sphere of my immediate life and surroundings.

As a mother today, I find myself naturally aspiring to follow in my mother's footsteps. These early years have been peppered with field trips that honor the emerging interests of my boys, particularly feeding Rowan's love of dinosaurs. And of course, my mother is there to nurture those interests too. One year she plotted a family trip to Dinosaur National Monument in Utah so we could visit the legendary Quarry Exhibit Hall. There visitors can view some 1,500 dinosaur bones preserved in a single rock wall. She even prepared for the trip by gifting Rowan with his own 'explorer's vest' and kit. He too is now on his way, his grandmother ushering him along in finding his passions and feeling his place in the large scheme of life.

Being Open to Mystery

I wanted to follow the leads of my boys and wander with them as they followed their interests and passions. How could I nurture an openness for experiencing awe and wonder? My children were there to remind me, and I too was there to remind them. When I was living from a place of awe or wonder, I was more available to surprise and mystery. I could be open to the unexpected twists of a day, the slow amble of an insect, the beauty of a rock, or the marvel of dinosaur tracks 100 million years old. I could model curiosity.

One of my favorite philosophers, Karl Jaspers, once wrote that his experience of the "Divine" was grounded in a "silence in the face of being." In silence, stillness and slowness, there are perhaps more opportunities for awe and wonder to arise. No hype, no "excitement," just pure, unadulterated silent observing. While things were often moving at top speed with my three boys, I wondered how I could foster these moments of pause throughout our days.

As Einstein says, "The most beautiful thing we can experience is the mysterious." How could I create the conditions for my children to relate to mystery? I often worried that my modern life was too highly structured. Were my kids getting enough time outdoors? Was I leaving enough space for the unexpected to arise? Today many of us have a highly structured public school system and an often over-scheduled agenda of after school activities. Was I cultivating enough time for silence and mystery, out of which awe and wonder more easily evolve?

As parents we can gently lay the groundwork for these unstructured, spontaneous moments. Nothing forced, nothing pressed. Only trusting that over time a culmination of shared moments and experiences may reveal this nugget of sweet, shared enjoyment of life—with a sense of the sacred and sublime forming the background, full of light.

The Invitation

Consider your own experience of awe or wonder.

When do you feel most alive and full of joy?

Do you take time to model awe and wonder in your own life?

Consider how you might weave in more space for silence and mystery in your family life.

Plan a spontaneous outing with your family.

Fostering Empathy

*"The purpose of human life is to serve,
and to show compassion and the will to help
others."*

~ Albert Schweitzer, Theologian and Philosopher

I grew up spending a lot of time at the churches where my father was a pastor. During the years when he worked as a Lutheran Campus Pastor at University of Illinois and Ohio State, there were often homeless people who would come to church, looking for help. My dad routinely treated them to coffee or lunch and gave them rides where they needed to be. My brother Rob and I would sit in the back seat, along for the ride—but also absorbing his example of generosity and kindness. On certain holidays, I'd join my dad at the soup kitchen to serve dinner, and when I went to college in Boston, I followed suit. There I worked for the Committee to End Elder Homelessness and volunteered for the overnight shift on weekends at the student-run homeless shelter at Harvard.

Ultimately, my dad planted the seeds of service. He, along with my mother, opened my eyes up enough to the condition of the world beyond my immediate home and community life that I was compelled to 'give back' where it was needed. My parents had given me all that I needed emotionally—and more. With this solid foundation, I had the capacity to care about life beyond myself. What they gave me transcended the basic human physical needs of food and shelter. They focused on providing quality time as a family and giving my brother and I their whole presence when we were together. They tended to our emotional well-being, always there to encourage and support. They guided. And they set amazing examples of how to live in the world with service to others as a guiding principle. As soon as I left home, I began seeking out ways to give back.

Following Dad's Footsteps

My dad had spent several years as a volunteer in Nigeria in the late 1960s, and I grew up hearing stories about his time there. He'd worked for the Red Cross during the Biafran Civil War. I had known from a young age that I wanted to follow in his footsteps. In fact, one of the reasons I chose to go to Boston University was their study abroad program in Niger, West Africa. I signed up to spend a semester in Niger, studying the social, economic and political challenges of Sub-Saharan Africa. One of the courses I took required a field placement in the community. I chose to work at the national hospital, where my eyes were opened to the painful reality of healthcare in what was then the poorest country on the planet. Those days were a confrontation with suffering: long lines of hundreds of women and children waiting for care, no running water, goats and cats parading around the hospital hallways, and a general dearth of resources.

After graduation I went back to West Africa as an international public health, water and sanitation volunteer with the Peace Corps in a small village in southern Mali. I focused on maternal and child healthcare, talking to mothers about nutrition at the local health center and biking to villages to weigh babies as part of a UNICEF campaign to reduce infant mortality. After my two years of service, I moved to Chicago and worked with a psycho-social rehabilitation organization as a mentor to at-risk youth. This work showed me the contrast of my own upbringing as I navigated the waters of teen mental health issues, gang pressure and violence, suicide attempts and eating disorders.

In more recent years, I've shifted my focus to environmental advocacy and sustainability education. I often reflect on my current status as a middle-class, European-American mother living a privileged life in Boulder, Colorado. My husband and I often grapple with how we can instill the values of empathy, compassion and service in our boys. I often feel our lifestyle is too good to be true. Here, the air is clean, the water flows from mountain tops, and open space and playgrounds abound. My kids are immersed in the arts and in contemplative education, eat healthy food, and play outside freely.

As a mother, I'm now focused on my small circle of influence, creating what I hope are the conditions for a safe and happy childhood. However, I also know that beyond my walls and commute to schools and the playground is a world mired in need. How, I wonder, do I bridge the gap?

How to Encourage Service?

The world too often seemed to be running amuck. What could I do here, now, with my three boys in order to make any difference? It was another invitation of motherhood. I chewed on this and had a hard time knowing where to start. Then it struck me:

empathy! *How could I parent in ways that open my children to the capacity for empathy?* Empathy moves us to care, and beyond caring is *acting. ?* Indeed, empathy may be critical to our collective survival.

I aspired to parent how my parents did. They cultivated an awareness of the world beyond my small orbit. At the same time, they also fostered the capacity for empathy that inspired me to tackle social work, public health and the environment. They had often gently reminded me of my own privilege and a responsibility to serve.

Now I too was tasked with raising a next generation of boys. I wanted to foster an open-minded and open-hearted connection to others (and to the natural world). My wish was that my children would care (deeply) about the world's problems and injustices. I knew that these roots could be nurtured at home. As a mother, I wanted nothing more than to raise children who would be happy, sensitive, responsible, sane and caring. And yet it often required going against the cultural grain of entitlement. Most days, it felt like an uphill battle.

During these early years of mothering, I'd focused on fostering human interaction and intimacy along with connection to nature. I'd tried to prioritize relating to people and the natural world more than relating to objects. I'd endeavored to model a slow pace amidst constant invitations to spin out into the cultural mania rooted in *more, faster, now.* We took deep breaths together. We slowed down. We slowed down again.

The Ground of Deep Connection

Perhaps most importantly, I could start by giving my children the ground of having their emotional needs met at home. I certainly didn't always succeed—but I tried. Not surprisingly, studies suggest that children are more likely to develop a strong sense of empathy when this is true. In her article on *Teaching Empathy: Evidence-Based Tips for Fostering Empathy in Children*, Dr. Gwen Dewar notes that children are more likely to show sympathy to others who are in distress when they have secure attachment relationships at home. From a secure and consistent ground of deep connection and trust, children can tune in more deeply to what is going on around them. So the simple day-to-day priority of being there for our children, listening to them, giving our full presence, and tending to all emotions arising lays this essential groundwork. These roots—or the absence of them—are influencing the world at large.

When Braeden came home from school one day recently, he wanted to talk about his friend intentionally squashing a ladybug. I knew this was a moment to pay close attention. How did he feel? What did he think about this choice? Why does a ladybug's life matter? Do ladybugs have families too? Over and over, Braeden wanted to know why his friend would do that. What did it mean to be dead? Why did these things happen?

Sweet & Sour = Lemonade: Be the Force Integrating All Sides

When I was five years old, I remember trying to come to terms with "bad" things. A first moment of realization came at a gas station. As my father was getting gas, I was standing right in line of the car exhaust of another car, blissfully breathing in the fumes. My dad of course quickly pulled me away, firmly telling me how bad it was for me. I was utterly dumbfounded. "But why do we use gas then in our cars if it isn't good for us?" I asked. My mind was blown open, and I was left very confused when he answered, "I don't know, sweetheart. That is a very good question..."

Later, my mother pulled out a children's book about how 'sweet plus sour makes lemonade.' This idea actually stayed with me as a perfect analogy for what it is like to be alive. I've even shared it with my own children, as a means for making sense of how the world is made up of so many contrasts. Yes, sweet plus sour makes the delicious combination of lemonade. Sour alone might not taste or feel good, but it contributes to the perfection of the final elixir. Light plus dark equals reality. Misfortune and love blend into a whole earth of complexity and fullness of human experience.

I wanted to open my children to this truth. But I realized it also required treading carefully. Yes, things could be confusing and difficult. Yes, bad things do happen sometimes. Yes, I wanted to keep cultivating pockets of "heaven" with my children and community. I wanted to contribute to an upbringing where compassion and creativity have a chance to flourish. But I also wanted to be ready to sit together in the unimaginable pain of the seemingly unexplainable. Rather than turning away, shutting down, running the other direction, or turning to distraction, I wanted to serve my children deeply by modeling a wide-awake disposition. How could I model empathy and kindness? How could I impart real wisdom about responding to the world's problems? It didn't only mean "doing more good" as much as *being* the force that represented the integration of all sides. And the heart is the crucible of ultimate integration.

Once this realization struck me, the invitation of motherhood then became helping my children learn to reside in the realm of the heart. There empathy could take root and the desire to serve could grow into a sense of purpose and responsibility. Feelings could be tended to—both my own as well as my children's. I could model living in ways that extended beyond my immediate circumference of familiarity. I could listen deeply and look for the learning moments, practicing openness and empathy myself.

The Invitation

When encountering a challenging moment or issue, notice your response.

Do you tend towards distraction? Do you shut down?

When do you notice yourself having the most empathy?

Consider ways to plant the seeds of service and empathy in your family.

Is there a project to undertake together? An issue to learn about?

Finding Silence & Simplicity in a World Moving Too Fast

"In the attitude of silence the soul finds the path in a clearer light, and what is elusive resolves itself into crystal clearness."

~ Mahatma Gandhi

As my children were growing up, I was working for the Northwest Earth Institute. It's a wonderful, small nonprofit offering resources that inspire people to connect, reflect and act on environmental issues. While at work, we often talk about how our programs offer a means of cutting through the vast cultural noise in order to distill what is important and then take action. One of my favorite course books published by the Northwest Earth Institute is titled *Voluntary Simplicity* (a newer edition of which is entitled *A Different Way: Living Simply in a Complex World*). I've long considered it an essential reference point for not only gauging the quality of my life, but whether I'm creating space for the things that matter most.

Duane Elgin, author of *The Living Universe,* is one of the leading writers on the practice of voluntary simplicity. He shares that at the heart of a simple life is an emphasis on harmonious and purposeful living. He says, "To live more voluntarily is to live more deliberately, intentionally and purposefully—in short, it is to live more consciously." He points out that it is difficult to be deliberate when we are also distracted. The aim of voluntary simplicity is to live in balance in order to find a life of greater purpose, fulfillment, and satisfaction.

What's Important? Creating Space

Since becoming a mother, it has been a long course in discerning how to create time and space for what's important. This includes both with my children as well as in my personal and professional life outside of my family. In Northwest Earth Institute's book *Voluntary Simplicity,* the focus is on the things that we consume, how we spend our time, what work we are doing in the world, and how our connection with nature is being nurtured or neglected.

As I gauged these realms in my own life, the Northwest Earth Institute helped me to stay on track. Each year I enlisted my family to join me in one of NWEI's annual EcoChallenges, and each October we would commit to trying on a new habit. Some years we focused on reducing our waste. Others we focused on driving less and biking more. One year we committed to taking care of the places we love by picking up trash, helping to keep our neighborhoods and parks clean. All this I hoped was helping us to create time and space for what's important.

The Upward Hill: Sugar & Screen Time

During the early years of parenting, I often had a recurring dream where I was biking up a long hill on a highway during winter at night. I was pedaling furiously, flanking the right side of the road. Meanwhile cars were flashing past me while sleet and snow blinded my vision. I always woke up feeling exhausted.

I'd been the only biker on the road. I knew I was trying to go my own way in the dream. I was trying to stay slow, even in spite of the fast cars overwhelming the scene. The dream pointed me towards what I often felt trying to keep up with daily responsibilities. All along, I was simultaneously trying to cultivate a simple lifestyle. There were often too many boundaries to set: too much sugar to say no to, too many opportunities for screen time, too many commitments, too much 'stuff,' too many toys...

In the realm of consumption, I was always struggling to strike a balance with eating less sugar and processed snacks. Sugar has infiltrated every crevice of American life. According to the United States Department of Agriculture's Economic Research Service, we consume on average 82 grams of sugar each day, or about 66 pounds of added sugar each year. And kids generally eat about 32 teaspoons of sugar a day, or three times the amount recommended by the American Heart Association. In spite of my best efforts, sugar seemed to be everywhere—and at kid eye level to boot.

And what about boundaries with screen time? According to the Kaiser Family Foundation, kids under age six watch an average of two hours of screen media a day, and kids and teens 8 to 18 years spend nearly four hours a day in front of a television screen and almost two additional hours on the computer or playing video games. Even when trying to avoid conforming to these statistics, the screens often infiltrated the backdrop of daily life, just like the sugar. At dinner out recently we counted six viewable screens. And there they were again at the coffee shop, and there they were again in the waiting room at the car wash.

Some days, I felt like I was losing control over the life I wanted to cultivate with my family. Screens and sugar seemed endless. Things moved so fast. Transitions abounded. How could I stand my ground? How could I resist the pressure to rush and be "busy"? How could I stay tuned in to what was important? How could I point my family to a different way?

Slowing Down

How did the dominant culture in America get to this place? A recent week of spring break at home with the kids reminded me of the slower rhythm possible in our mornings when we weren't bound by the clock. Time could slow down a bit, more mindfulness prevailed. In general, there was a bit more silence. Our schedule was simple and uncluttered. We were spontaneous. We could take more time to notice and take joy in the little things, too. I liked it. Immensely.

Artist and poet Jean Arp says, *"Soon silence will have passed into legend. We've turned our backs on silence. Day after day humans invent machines and devices that increase noise and distract humanity from the essence of life, contemplation, meditation...*

The inhuman void spreads monstrously like a gray vegetation."

This image of gray vegetation stayed with me. It resonated. It was this "gray vegetation" that I was reckoning with as I raised my children. It was the "gray vegetation" of a life with too few pauses and too much stimuli of all kinds. All of the sudden the experience of life could too easily become the blur of scenery flying by on a road. Everything could look the same everywhere we went because we weren't close enough, or slow enough, to notice subtlety. In this scenario, what if we were missing the quiet, simple beauty of the lone flower peeking out in spring under snow? What if we were missing the "good stuff" of life each day?

The absence of silence felt intimately connected to the difficulty in finding what Elgin would call "harmonious and purposeful living." The rushing to be anywhere "on time," the extreme sweet foods and the screens everywhere I went combined to form a cocktail of madness that swirled like a hum underneath it all. And yet I knew I could choose to live in this swirl with as much slowness and intentionality as possible. I could set boundaries that worked for my family. I could say "there is no rush" over and over again.

I started trying on a few more new habits. When I was with the children, I tried to keep my phone on airplane mode. In the car, I turned the radio off. I practiced taking deep breaths while driving. I made a point to notice the details of the trees along the road. I focused on the important gifts that can be given as a parent—the gift of quality time, full, engaged presence, silence as the backdrop as often as possible, and the freedom of no agenda when we are able.

Prioritizing Simplicity & Silence

Prioritizing simplicity and silence felt like the antidote to a culture often moving too fast. How could I integrate more time outside? More time getting lost in the small details of nature? More art and movement? More quality time with friends and less running around on the fly with granola bars gobbled in the back seat? Perhaps most importantly, how could I take the time needed to clarify what was most important? How did I want to organize my days? What were my priorities and how was I living them? I had to remember, again and again, that I do have agency in how I live my life and how I raise my children. Even though it can feel as if we are pulled into a very fast cultural stream, we can still swim like a turtle—carrying a home where there is always the possibility of finding stillness and silence in a world full of noise.

The Invitation

Consider what is most important in your life.

How are you creating space for the things that matter most?

Where would you like to cultivate more balance?

Identify one or two areas where you can begin.

What Do the Grandmothers Say?

*"Our deeds travel with us from afar,
and what we have been makes us what we
are..."*

~ Mary Anne Evans (also known as George Eliot),
English Novelist and Poet

Long before becoming a mother, I was an avid family genealogist. As a child I was always asking my parents questions about their lives and their families, eager to know where my grandparents had come from and what had drawn them to Cleveland, Ohio and Chicago, Illinois. The interest deepened during my time in West Africa, where the oral traditions are strong and where many people can offer up a detailed history of who their ancestors were and the path that they traveled. Perhaps it was because so much was unknown in my family story that I wanted to know more. Or perhaps it was because I was a somewhat 'typical' European American with roots spanning the globe. I wanted to understand my own cultural identity.

I set out on what has now become a 20 year journey into my family history, reconnecting with the stories and roots of the McNamaras of County Clare, Ireland, the Billington seamen of England and Norway, the Grabowskys of central Poland, the Zachs and Lembkes of eastern Germany, and the countless other family lines who migrated over the centuries in search of a better life—converging in my birth in

Oklahoma City, 1976. What struck me was that in an overwhelming majority of instances my ancestors had left their homelands to flee poverty or persecution. Perhaps this explained my experience of loss: loss of culture, loss of sense of place, loss of oral traditions and family stories handed down over time.

When I became a mother, my investment in knowing my roots deepened. Suddenly I could sense the continuum of my lifespan as being part of a much vaster progression. My life wasn't just my life. I was now part of a long thread of mothers and sons and mothers and daughters spanning time. I was one link in a very long chain. I wanted to share stories from this long tapestry of varied history with my children. I started picking different threads of history to tell my boys for their bedtime stories.

My sons were struck by even the simplest of stories, especially the ones that related to the great grandparents who they inherited their last name from. Where was Italy? How long of a boat ride would it have been to get to America? How old was Papa's grandpa when he had to leave his home? Slowly over the years I weaved the stories in. It engendered a curiosity. Out of the blue, Rowan would ask me: "Mama, remind me - am I more Italian in my blood or more Irish?"

Storylines from the Family Tree

Over the years I found myself thinking a lot about my great, great grandmother, Katherine McCabe McNamara, whose family hailed from County Cavan, Ireland. Perhaps her story struck me because, like me, she was mother to three boys. I even found a photograph of her, dressed in black, standing right behind my great, great, great grandparents John and Eliza McCabe. The family arrived in America in the mid 1800's, likely one of the millions of immigrants fleeing the potato famine in Ireland. They settled in Campbell and Bath, New York. Kate eventually married my great, great grandfather John Charles McNamara, who left her a widower in 1905.

For some reason she has stayed with me. Perhaps it is because I can see a bit of myself in her expression in the single photo I have. Perhaps it is because she gets me thinking about how in our present-moment family lives we are still a continuation of a very large family tree. Each time a new child is welcomed into the family, the DNA from thousands of ancestors and places culminate in my story, and each baby's story. Each time I gave birth the mothers before me would appear in my imagination. Their journeys live on in the form of story.

Even though women's stories are focused on less in the annals of history, the small remnants of their lives peek through. Some of my grandmothers traveled across oceans during tumultuous times. One carved her name in the crypt at Canterbury where persecuted Protestants worshipped. Several fled the potato famine and ended up in crowded boarding houses in Brooklyn, working in the carpet factories. When I consider the span of time during which these grandmothers were alive, days suddenly aren't just days—they are instead the culmination of thousands of years of evolution, genealogy and history. Days aren't just days—they are the ongoing writing of deep, rooted storylines, weaving pattern lines on my skin, my children's skin, right here.

Curating Family Stories

In Henry Wadsworth Longfellow's poem *The Day Is Done*, he points to "the bards sublime, whose distant footsteps echo through the corridors of time." In Ireland, the bards or poets historically played an important role, filling the office of both historian and genealogist. They curated the stories and signposts of a family or clan, recording and sharing them across generations, handing us the artifacts that pointed to the significant impressions made over time. In this way, culture and identity were transmitted. Where we came from and where we have been was deemed of utmost importance.

In today's very different world, we as parents can still play these vital roles, reminding our children of the larger spans of lifetimes. We can help to put our current lives in perspective and context. We can share the information we deem important for posterity. The stories we tell can inspire respect for those who have passed before us, and a sense of awe and mystery in the face of where we have come from and where we are going. What survives over centuries? What traits do we inherit from those we've never met but who we are related to? How do we maintain vital connections to our past while also shaping our future? What legacy do we as individuals, families and societies wish to leave behind? Are we telling the stories we want to hand down? Is there time for remembering the long-term perspective of our lives? What are we growing in this lifetime? What are the roots? What is worth preserving and upholding across the vast annals of time?

What Will Survive? What Is Important?

So what would the grandmothers say? They remind me that each lifetime is but a blink. Birth. Childbirth. Marriage. Death. These are often the key signposts of a life that remain in the records of history. The grandmothers remind me to take the 'long' perspective: seeing beyond any given moment into the vast continuum of life. They remind me to marvel at what has survived. They remind me of the preciousness of each of our individual life stories. And, finally, they remind me to confront my own mortality. They have come and gone and so will we all.

What will survive? What is important? These are the questions I ask as I navigate each day with my family. What can we as mothers leave for the future? What do we want to focus on so we can live more fully into 'the good stuff?' Yes! Stories. Yes! Meaningful traditions. Yes! Simple moments of connection and presence. Yes! Cultivating awe. Yes! Acts of kindness. Yes! Practicing love, even in the difficult moments.

My grandmother Rhea passed away at age 91. During my last visit with her, she was breathing through a tube of oxygen. She was still poised, a paragon of loveliness in the midst of terminal lung cancer. My youngest son Kienan joined me on a trip to see her for a final visit at her home in South Carolina. He was only nine months old at the time, but he got to non-verbally absorb the history and felt experience that is unique to each family. My mom, dad, brother, nephew and aunt were all with her as well. We all sat together in the smallest room of the house, surrounded by photographs.

Family stories abounded, accompanied by the emotional undertones and overtones reminiscent of a life full of everything: birth and death, the dramas, the pain, the hurt feelings, the love, the mistakes, the brightness, the seasons of youth, the tragedies, the years of habit and routine, the joys and kindness, the shadow and the light. Photos from the 1959 vacation to Mexico were unearthed. The scrapbook from Grandma's 90th birthday celebration. Grandpa's album from World War II and Iwo Jima. The photos from the last family reunion. Baby photos from the births of each of my sons. Happy memories were knitted together with sad musings about my grandpa's final days. "Remember those pancakes he used to make on Saturdays?" "Remember the failed tapioca pudding recipe?" Everyone laughed.

My aunt cooked up a feast and my brother asked my grandmother what wisdom she would like to share for us younger ones. Without missing a beat she replied, *"Just keep loving...Just keep loving."* Yes, indeed. My grandmother had reminded me of the greatest invitation of them all.

The Invitation

*Consider your life story and this moment
in your life as a mother.*

Hold the perspective of your long family history.

What has survived?

*What do you want to preserve or uphold with your
children in this lifetime?*

What might your own grandmothers say?

*What do you want to focus on so you can live more
fully into 'the good stuff?'*

*As you finish this book, create time and space for
reflection – allowing glimmers of new possibilities to
emerge.*

Invite new practices to take root.

*And as my grandmother said,
Remember: "Just keep loving!"*

Epilogue

"It is the most distant course that comes nearest to thyself, and that training is the most intricate which leads to the utter simplicity of a tune.

The traveler has to knock at every alien door to come to her own, and one has to wander through all the outer worlds to reach the innermost shrine at the end..."

- Rabindranath Tagore, *The Journey Home*

As a mother, I've had many a moment where I've felt like a scuba diver needing to come up to the surface. Some months I don't even realize I've been submerged, swimming through my days which turn into months and then years. Writing helps me to resurface and reflect—and when I do, I'm always amazed at what emerges.

Writing this book has been the ultimate reflection on my life journey and how the path of motherhood has fit in. What have the lessons been? How have I grown and changed? When my oldest son turned eight, I came across the Tagore poem above and it reminded me to consider my journey through life in a spiritual context. How was I leaving my track, especially with my family and my children? How was I (or wasn't I) "coming into my own?" How had motherhood shaped me, nearly a decade in?

As this book goes to print, I'm noting how one phase of parenting (and childhood) closes while another opens. So it is with life. Each transition provides the opportunity to consider lessons learned. Did I soak in the sweet moments of cuddles enough? Have I appreciated the times when I have simply held hands with my children? Was I too firm at times? Did I do all the things I'd dreamed of doing during these precious early years? Life and all its moving parts are continually shifting, reminding me to embrace it *now*.

As I look back at the period of time during which this book was written, I can acknowledge that my identity has fully settled into something I could never have imagined when I was pregnant with my first son. Many months and years have indeed felt like 'knocking at alien doors'—the sleepless nights, the unsettledness of shifting body and personal identity, the new worries, the unchartered responsibilities. It has been a strange wandering at times, often treading new waters that have forced me out of my comfort zone and spread me thinner than the flattest of pancakes.

I remember when I first embarked on the path of motherhood. I was newly pregnant and I'd been sitting across my husband over dinner at a Thai restaurant, telling him that I wanted to "induct a meaningful human experience." I'd wanted to walk the path of Big Love. It all sounded—and felt—so idealistic then. It was before big messes and frayed nervous systems. It was before the chaos.

The traveler has to knock at every alien door to come to her own, and one has to wander through all the outer worlds to reach the innermost shrine at the end.

What *is* the *innermost shrine at the end?* And how does the motherhood journey circle there? The lessons that want to shine through are like little gifts on an altar. I only see them when I take the scuba mask off and look towards the light dancing on water at the surface. They indeed are like reminders on the journey—signposts that are meant to bring us home to ourselves again and again.

The word shrine comes from the Old English *scrin*, referring to a 'cabinet, chest or reliquary.' I imagine a place where I store my most treasured items. This place serves as a reminder of what I most want to remember. It is here where I can tuck away the deepest lessons for safekeeping. For me, this place holds a reminder to remember to dip into my own inner life, to take the time to digest my experience through introspection. It holds a reminder to also not get lost amidst all the responsibilities and competing demands for my time and attention. It holds a reminder to make room for the meaningful, and about appreciation for what is, exactly. It reminds me about the deep and vast power of love.

At 3:42am on June 15, 2017, the phone rang by my head. I was in a deep sleep, sandwiched between two of my sons. It was my brother urging me to get to his house pronto. Baby was on the way. I could hear my sister-in-law in labor in the background and I knew I better be quick. I was slated to be with my little nephew Lundin while baby was being born. I'd been sleeping with my phone by the bed for several weeks, waiting for this very call.

I reached their home a few minutes later, quietly opening the front door to find that I'd arrived before the midwife and baby was already crowning. He'd come faster than anyone could have imagined and the midwife was still dodging her way across town to be there. I tripped up the stairs while running as fast as I could, willing myself to be as wakeful as possible. In the darkness, I could see that my brother was supporting my new nephew's head as he was coming into the world. Just as I took my place, his eyes and part of his nose emerged. My brother and I looked at each other with the widest of eyes. Time stood still. My senses sharpened. "Is this really happening?" I remember thinking. Even my sister-in-law said it felt like a dream.

Here I was again at a birth, coming full circle in a way. As Orion Robert McNamara was born with one final push into my brother's hands, I remembered back to my own births. I was now at a different vantage point, able to pay homage to my sister-in-law as she fearlessly birthed her son in unexpected and unimagined circumstances. Indeed, just as I'd pondered during the birth of my own first child, it was the continued cycle of life landing in our arms— *a gift so precious we often call it a miracle.*

In the moments that followed, my brother wrapped Orion carefully and placed him on my sister-in-law's belly. I jumped on the phone with the midwife who was on her way, and listened as she talked us through what to do to ensure that baby was safe and healthy. The adrenaline was pumping and I was admittedly more nervous than I'd ever been in my entire life. "Is there anything else we should be doing?" I asked breathlessly after it was clear that Orion was a strong and perfectly healthy newborn.

"Yes," said the midwife. "Tell Rob and Brooke to just fall in love with their child."

Just. Fall. In. Love.

The midwife had been able to peer through the adrenaline, the worries, the commotion and wonder to distill this most important advice. Baby and mother were safe and well. Now: Just. Fall. In. Love. We all smiled as we settled into the mystery of what had just transpired. It was 3:49am.

As I watched these first precious moments of greeting one another and bonding, I sat back to take stock of what a blessing it was to be there. The motherhood journey had thrown its curve ball of unpredictability, once again inviting forth an exquisite and beautiful path.

Acknowledgements

This creative project would not have been possible were it not for the members of my most amazing family. Thank you to my own mother and father, Robert Patrick McNamara Jr. and Joan Ellen Lundin McNamara for bringing into existence a family unit that was full of love and support, mutual appreciation and the cultivation of deep thinking, wonder, reflection, endless fun, adventure and gratitude.

Thank you to my husband and partner in life, Christopher Peraro—and to my three sons, Rowan, Braeden and Kienan, all of whom have shown me new layers of love and connection and have been my constant, steady companions day in and day out in all things. Having children and cultivating my own family has been one of the greatest experiences of my lifetime, and I'm infinitely grateful to each of you for all the ways in which you teach me the greatest lessons of life.

Thank you to my brother, Robert Lundin McNamara, for your support and inspiration in my creative and spiritual journeys. Since you were born, you've always been a bright light in my life and I love the ways in which our paths have remained close and connected over the span of our lifetime! Thank you for blazing the way with your own book writing, and for helping to make this book possible through much practical and logistical publishing support. I love you beyond infinity, brother!

Thank you to my sister-in-law Brooke Gessay McNamara, who is a bright, creative force and like a true sister in my life. Thank you for the guidance and support along the way! And to my sweet nephews Lundin and Orion, who continue to shower our family with blessings and sweetness.

Thank you to my editor Robin Quinn, who tirelessly edited this manuscript with great attention to detail and with a keen eye for improvement. Thank you too to authors Karen Maezen Miller and Betsy Henry who offered up early advice when this book was only a seed.

Thank you to those of you who supported me in so many ways in making this vision a reality. You are not all listed here but you know who you are. Thank you! To Kelli Kessler May, Nina Hausfeld, Devon Corbet, Ellen Boeder and Tara Deubel, who were all early readers and offered invaluable feedback. To Leigh Meislann Dennis for publishing and writing advice. To Anja Apitz, Blythe Massey and Amy Desautels-Stein for early encouragement on my 39th birthday when I committed to this project. To Jackie MacNeish, Angie Kochukudy, Amy Desautels-Stein and Amy Delaterre for detailed input on the cover design. To Jenny Lynch for self-publishing advice. And thank you to each of you amazing women who meet with me on the third Thursday of each month in Boulder, and for all the evenings spent clarifying our visions and intentions and sharing the intimate details of our lives. Thank you too to the 'Group Afo' ladies (you know who you are!). The support and inspiration of these groups over the years has been invaluable.

I also offer a deep bow of gratitude to Parenting Educator and Coach Miriam Mason Martineau, who did not know me but still offered her early support and encouragement and who graciously wrote the foreword for this book. Thank you for your work supporting and inspiring so many parents through your writing, your classes and your work.

Finally, I want to thank the teachers and staff of Alaya Preschool in Boulder, Colorado. My children have attended this school collectively for over seven years, and the presence of this unique school rooted in contemplative practices and education has been a huge source of support and guidance over these early years of parenting. Thank you for gifting the community with a sacred space where our children can truly flourish.

These acknowledgements would not be complete without a final gesture of thanks to Hatha yoga teacher Sofia Diaz, who I had the great honor of studying with for many years and whose teachings are reflected throughout this book.

With gratitude,
Deborah McNamara

Boulder, Colorado
Spring, 2018